To Cliff with
best wishes,
T.N
27.1.93.

THE LION AND THE LAMB

The Lion and the Lamb

Figuralism and Fulfilment in the Bible, Art and Literature

TIBOR FABINY
Lecturer in English Literature
Attila Jozsef University, Budapest

St. Martin's Press   New York

© Tibor Fabiny 1992

All rights reserved. For information, write:
Scholarly and Reference Division,
St. Martin's Press, Inc., 175 Fifth Avenue,
New York, N.Y. 10010

First published in the United States of America in 1992

Printed in Hong Kong

ISBN 0-312-07544-8

Library of Congress Cataloging-in-Publication Data
Fabiny, Tibor.
The lion and the lamb : figuralism and fufilment in the Bible,
art, and literature / Tibor Fabiny.
   p.   cm.—(Studies in literature and religion)
Includes bibliographical references (p.   ) and index.
ISBN 0-312-07544-8
1. Typology (Theology) 2. Typology (Linguistics)
3. Hermeneutics.   4. Religion and literature.   5. Art and religion.
I. Title.   II. Series.
BS478.F28   1992
220.6'4—dc20   91-34612
                                                                CIP

For Delinke and Félix-Péter

Contents

List of Plates		ix
General Editor's Preface		x
Preface		xi
1	Introduction	1
	What is Typology or Figuralism	1
	Northrop Frye and the Rediscovery of Typology	4
	The Risk of Typology	10
2	The Hermeneutical Context	13
	Language: from Figure to Fulfilment	13
	Meaning: from Seed to Plant	26
	Reading: Eating the Book	39
3	Reading Scripture	45
	The Unity of Scripture	45
	Typology in the Old Testament	47
	Typology in the New Testament	58
	The Lion and the Lamb (The Apocalypse)	73
4	Reading Pictures	78
	Visual Exegesis – *Pictura Quasi Scriptura*	78
	Reading Medieval Typological Programmes	85
	The Klosterneuburg Altar	87
	The Biblia Pauperum	92
	The *Speculum Humanae Salvationis*	103
	The Impact of the Typological Vision on Medieval Art	108
5	Reading Literature	111
	From Prefiguration to Postfiguration	111
	Dramatic Hermeneutics in the 'Abraham and Isaac' Play of the Chester–cycle (Pagina IV)	115

'Like Power Divine' – Figuration and Meta-drama
   in Shakespeare's *Measure for Measure*   122
Fulfilment of the 'Eternal Design' in
   T. S. Eliot's *Murder in the Cathedral*   131
Conclusion: The Figure Fulfilled   136

Notes   138

Bibliography   150

Index   159

List of Plates

1. *Biblia Pauperum*. Magi (centre), Abner before David (left), Sheba before Solomon (right).

2. *Biblia Pauperum*. Egyptian Idols Fall (centre), Golden Calf (left), Dagon Falls (right).

3. *Biblia Pauperum*. The Jews Fall Back (centre), Foolish Girls Condemned (left), Fall of Angels (right).

4. *Speculum Humanae Salvationis*. Christ Prays for his Torturers, Tubalcain and Jubal, The Martyrdom of Isaias, Moab Sacrifices his Son.

General Editor's Preface

Tibor Fabiny describes the purpose of this book as 'to establish a theory of typology on the basis of reader-response criticism'. As he so richly demonstrates, 'typology' is at once a simple notion – the linking in art and literature of type with antitype – and yet profound and elusive. His discussion embraces numerous aspects of the relationship between literature and religion, from biblical criticism, to attention given to a broad tradition of literature and art, and finally to contemporary literary theory.

Above all this study is profoundly theological. It interweaves the language and images of the Christian tradition with a sense of the on-going, questing nature of its faith at every level of popular imagination and intellectual enquiry. Its theme is salvation history in the foundational literature of the Old and New Testaments, and in the dramatic literature of Western theatre.

Like many other books in this series, Fabiny's work is also concerned with hermeneutics and interpretation. For the problems and life of hermeneutics lie at the heart of typology, and link it with the central preoccupations of contemporary criticism – textuality and intertextuality, language and rhetoric.

Good criticism should always encourage the reader to return and re-read the great texts of a religious tradition and its literature. This is precisely what this book does, for it is all about the act of reading. As an encouragement to read the Bible in the light of medieval drama, Shakespeare and T. S. Eliot, and vice versa, it lies centrally within the preoccupations and purposes of the study of literature, art and religion.

DAVID JASPER

Preface

Martin Luther is recorded in his *Table-Talk* as saying that 'the multitude of books is a great evil. There is no measure or limit to this fever of writing. Everybody must be an author; some out of vanity, to acquire celebrity and raise up a name, others for the sake of lucre and gain. The Bible is now buried under so many commentaries that the text is nothing regarded. I could wish all my books were buried nine ells deep in the ground, by reason of the ill example they will give, everyone seeking to imitate me in writing many books with the hope of procuring fame.'

Having these straightforward and peculiarly contemporary words in mind I must give a rather apologetic explanation for the existence of this book. On what grounds can the present book be justified amongst the 'multitude of books', or even the contemporary dilution of writing?

First of all, it must be admitted that writing a book, especially if it is going to be your first, is indeed, just as Luther said, a feverish activity with great responsibility and of course, an intellectual challenge. You write because you feel that you can offer something from a particular perspective. My perspective on the Bible is that of the literary critic and that of the reader with some theological background. Moreover, when you write you mayt feel that you have something to say, to communicate or share with others, and it is thrilling to envisage the invisible community of readers who are engaged in a dialogue with you whether or not you might ever hear what they are saying or thinking. Each book is a lonely monologue only in its initial phase because it hopes to encourage, or perhaps even provoke, discussion. Each book is completed by the reader. Its primary aim is to evoke response and the question whether the reader agrees or disagrees with the author, is only a secondary issue. Dialogue is the sign of life, therefore orality, as Walter Ong said, precedes textuality: all text is pretext. And if the author happens to have been brought up behind a certain curtain, say in Eastern Europe, where quite frequently the very access to books has been regarded as a scholarly achievement, then it is perhaps even more understandable that now, with the walls demolished and the curtain raised, he is pleased to have been given the opportunity to share some of his ideas with the invisible community of his readers. Therefore I am most grateful to David Jasper, the General Editor of the series 'Studies in Literature and Religion' for inviting me to contribute to that.

However, the apology should not be primarily that of the author but rather of the subject-matter. What is the rationale for writing a book on biblical typology or figuralism today? Probably the term 'biblical typology' does not strike the reader as a fashionable topic. If it is given any thought at all then it is usually assumed to be bound up with a precritical, fanciful exercise worthy only of an antiquarian investigation. One of my purposes is to show that things are often different from how they seem and a critical and scholarly inquiry can help us to question our own images of things in order to arrive at a new and fresh understanding.

I do not aspire to revive a traditional, dogmatic view of typology. Traditionally, typology has been seen as a part of the divine revelation. It is not my concern either to affirm or to challenge this position. I only wish to claim that typology makes sense to me. I hope to show that it is not only 'prefiguration' but also 'postfiguration' as *typos* is both *Vorbild* and *Nachbild*. Therefore typology embraces the questions of imitation (I am using the word in the sense of Kempis' *imitatio*), obedience, completion and, above all, fulfilment. Most of my thoughts in the following pages will revolve around the nature and meaning of fulfilment. I shall advocate the view that art can also be seen as fulfilment.

Many significant books have already been written about typology but in order to justify my claim I have to adopt a relatively new approach, at least from two aspects. First, I place typology in the context of reader-response criticism, because I find that typology, amongst other things, is primarily a way of reading. Since Gadamer we have known that the art of understanding (*ars intelligendi*) cannot be separated from the art of application (*ars applicandi*): I understand the text only if I am involved in it, if I apply its validity to me. Robert Jauss' reception-aesthetics and Wolfgang Iser's idea of the implied reader' and his reader-response criticism are based on this assumption. This is exactly what happens in typology: the reader finds himself, or herself, absorbed by the text and by identifying himself or herself with the text, he recreates it. My thesis is that typology is reading and reading is both a recreation of the text and a recreation of the reader.

The other unusual feature of my project is its consciously

comprehensive and interdisciplinary nature. This is not a book for purists. Typology is, by its nature, a very complex phenomenon and its aspects have been discussed by theologians, literary critics and art historians. But I find that a comprehensive treatment of this phenomenon is still lacking. For me art and literature can always reveal some new, so far unrecognized, aspects of typology. I was fascinated to learn new insights on typology from biblical scholars like Goppelt or Gerhard von Rad, from patristic experts like Daniélou or Henri de Lubac, from art historians like Peter Bloch or George P. Landow and, of course, from literary historians and critics such as Erich Auerbach, A. C. Charity or Northrop Frye. I very much enjoy the company of these scholars, sitting around the same table discussing the same subject matter from their own scholarly or critical perspective. I wondered, therefore, how to share this recognition with my readers. Writing a synthesizing treatise on 'Typology in Scripture, Art and Literature' would have been too ambitious a project and such an enterprise would have demanded several more years of research from me and probably encyclopedic volumes from a publisher. But it is my hope that reader-response criticism has made my intended comprehensive discussion of the subject possible. And so, after elaborating a hermeneutical theory of reading I shall discuss my subject as 'Reading Scripture', 'Reading Pictures' and 'Reading Literature'. With a selection of readings as case-studies I can preserve my original comprehensive project, embracing the Bible, as well as iconography and literature. I am aware that my excursions into at least three disciplines may have their concomitant dangers but the sole 'hero' whom I accompany to various domains in the following pages is, typology. As I am not a biblical scholar I shall rely heavily on the works of Leonard Goppelt, Gerhard von Rad, Oscar Cullmann or D. L. Baker in my discussion of the biblical material. I hope that such a comprehensive and reading-oriented approach will also yield some new insights for my readers.

As for the theological discussion of typology, Leonard Goppelt's *Typos* (first published in 1939) is still the classic. In literary criticism the most significant monograph was published twenty five years ago by A. C. Charity (*Events and Their Afterlife*, 1966). But I am particularly indebted to the works of Northrop Frye most of whose books, as I hope to show in my introduction, though not explicitly devoted to the subject, have revolved around typology. Therefore, I hope, his presence will be felt throughout my book.

Earlier drafts or chapters of my manuscript were read by Kevin Keith, Linda Munk, Istvan Szabo and Marc Vervenne. Chapters of the final version were read by Bridget Nichols, Carol Harrison and Gordon Jeanes. The whole manuscript was read by David Jasper. I owe thanks to their perceptive insights and critical remarks but the responsibility for all the errors is mine. My thanks are due to Alison Jasper for her hard labour of polishing my style. I am grateful to Dr Linda Munk for making her unpublished manuscript 'The Seamless Garment: for Northrop Frye' available to me.

Now, with a retrospective view I find a 'shadowy prefiguration' of the present book in an anthology that I compiled and edited for publication by Attila József University, Szeged in 1988. The design of this larger enterprize has been on my mind ever since. The following pages were completed during the academic year 1989–90 and the autumn term of 1990–91. I am grateful to the Department of English at Attila József University, Hungary for generously allowing me an extended study-leave of fifteen months during which time I was able to work in the excellent library of the Theological Faculty of the Catholic University of Leuven, Belgium with a grant from the Soros Foundation and the Research Council of the University. I was more than privileged to receive two short-term fellowships as having been awarded a Northrop Frye Fellowship at Victoria University of the The University of Toronto, Canada in April 1990. I gained a great deal from my stimulating discussions with Dr Northrop Frye, who reminded me to keep the comprehensive nature of my project 'in my mind' and to be selective in my writing. I was also honoured to be offered a Macmillan Fellowship for the Michaelmas Term of the academic year 1990–91 at the Centre for the Study of Literature and Theology, at St Chad's College in The University of Durham. This Centre has proved to be an ideal academic community in which I could complete my book. Versions of Chapter 2 of this book were given as public lectures in Toronto and Durham. I owe thanks and gratitude to all these institutions for making the writing of this book possible.

But my gratitude, above all, is due to my family, my wife Delinke and our two-year-old son Félix-Péter (who shared in particular, my enthusiasm in reading the *Biblia Pauperum*). Both of them patiently put up with my absence from the joys and duties of family life. In some slight compensation, this book is dedicated to them.

1

Introduction

WHAT IS TYPOLOGY OR FIGURALISM?

Literary critics who endeavour to read *The Great Code*, Northrop Frye's monograph on the Bible and Literature (1982), might be somewhat puzzled when first confronting its Table of Contents. Four words constitute the architectural pillars of this book: 'language', 'metaphor', 'myth' and 'typology'. The first three words belong to the everyday vocabulary of a literary scholar but he might find the fourth word odd and curious: 'typology'. Provided he is of an inquisitive mind he might cautiously and silently raise the question: 'What then, is typology?'

This book aims at answering this simple question and the following pages are meant to invite the reader on an excursion into an intellectual no man's land, a territory shared by biblical scholars, literary critics and art historians. Right at the beginning of this journey I wish to voice my suspicion that perhaps the future conquerors of this land will be those who are interested in language – namely, in the creative and recreative power of words. Unprejudiced, honest inquiry, artistic sensitivity and some intellectual patience are required from those who are willing to undertake this voyage.

It is difficult to provide a brief and concise definition of typology or figuralism. (As the Latin equivalent of the Greek *typos* is *figura*, scholars have frequently tended to use the term 'figuralism' instead of 'typology' and therefore I am also using these terms as synonyms). Indeed, the elusive nature of typology seems to resist any attempt to force a narrow definition. The word typology may denote various activities, principles or aspects of language. However, whatever these activities, principles or aspects may be, they are all related to the Bible, particularly to the Christian Bible that has been a major informing source of Western culture. If we tried to take into account everything typology may refer to, we could enumerate at least nine various 'things': (1) a way of reading the Bible; (2) a principle of unity of the 'Old' and the 'New' Testaments in the Christian Bible; (3) a principle of exegesis; (4) a figure of speech; (5) a mode of thought; (6) a form of rhetoric; (7) a vision of history; (8) a principle of artistic composition; (9) a manifestation of 'intertextuality'.

If we have all the complexity of the word in mind then the traditional understanding of typology will probably be seen to be reductive. Nevertheless we have to take this traditional understanding into account too if we want to take a step further. In the traditional and most commonly understood sense, the word typology was used when certain real or supposedly historical events, persons or 'things' in the Old Testament were seen as being, in addition, prefigurative symbols – that is, 'types' of which the 'fulfilment' or 'reality' was given in the New Testament in the form of so-called 'antitypes'. Thus the crossing of Jordan (an event) is a type of baptism, Joshua (person) is a type of Jesus and the manna (a thing) is a type of the Lord's Supper.

But this traditional and common understanding of typology lacks accuracy from at least two aspects. First, we cannot bluntly state that typology is confined only to the relationship of the two testaments of the Christian Bible because, as we shall see, the typological mode of thought is already present in the Old Testament. In Deutero-Isaiah, for example, God appears to create 'new' out of the 'old' as he himself is both 'steadfast' and 'new'. The prophecies emphasize throughout that there are typical events (such as the Exodus), there are typical individuals (Moses is the prophet *par excellence*, Aaron is the type of priesthood, David is the typical king), or typical places (Jerusalem or Zion has from the very beginning been seen as the eschatological type of 'being saved', while Babylon, on the other hand, has been interpreted as the eschatological type of God's Judgement). Thus some concrete (or sometimes only supposedly) historical events, persons, or places were elevated to the rank of the symbol and whoever or whatever lived up to this symbol was seen as a Moses or David or Elijah *redivivus*, a new person, event, place or thing was seen as 'filling in' the frame of the prototypical person, event, place or thing. This 'filling in' or 'filling full' of the 'frame' was seen as 'fulfilment'. We shall return to this dialectic shortly, when we turn to the linguistic aspects of typology.

The second deficiency of the traditional understanding of typology suggested by the above definition is that it gives the impression that typology is a living issue only for theologians and biblical scholars. The present situation is, in fact, exactly the reverse. Today typology is a dead letter in theology. It is, as Northrop Frye says, 'a neglected subject . . . because it is assumed to be bound up with a doctrinaire adherence to Christianity.'[1] Due to this prejudice and the lack of a fresh understanding, typology has only sporadically been able to break into the mainstream trends of theology (for example, Von Rad) and therefore it has been doomed to survive mainly in some sub-theological and fundamentalist circles. Modern and enlightened theologians, mistakenly I think, still tend to assign it to a dusty, odd, precritical naivite. My thesis is, however, that with a fresh look at the creative dynamics of biblical language, with a new understanding of 'what is a text?' and with a perceptive attention to the strategies of 'intertextuality' within the Bible, we might arrive at a 'postcritical' affirmation and appropriation of typology.

So theologians tend to be silent about typology. The curious phenomenon today is that the discussion of typology has been taken over by secular scholars: literary critics, art-historians or historians, such as Erich Auerbach, A. C. Charity, Barbara Kiefer Lewalski, Frank Kermode, George P. Landow, P. J. Korshin and, above all, by Northrop Frye.[2] One cannot but be surprised by the theologians' silence on typology when one recognizes that this originally biblical mode of thought has been converted into a massive cultural tradition. This tradition is manifest in medieval iconography (we can associate the 'speaking' cathedral windows, or the 'preaching' *Biblia Pauperum*), in medieval drama (for example, the mystery-cycles of Abraham and Isaac). Friedrich Ohly has done magnificent scholarly research on the interrelationship of theology, art and history-writing in the Middle Ages, on how the pattern of the logic of biblical typology was extended into half-biblical or extra-biblical typology especially in medieval secular poetry.[3] The typological tradition is conspicuously present in English literature: it is adopted by the metaphysical poets, Milton, or by the Pre-Raphaelite poets and painters of the nineteenth century. Other scholars – like Perry Miller, Ursula Brumm, Sacvan Bercovitch, Mason I. Lowance – have published a great number of books demonstrating how biblical typology has formulated the American identity and consciousness since the time of the Pilgrim Fathers.[4] We have to bear in mind that all ideas about the new world as opposed to the 'old': 'New' York, 'New' Jersey and so on, go back to the typological perception of God's recreating of the 'old'. This unceasing divine activity, according to the Bible, will culminate in the recreation of the world which brings about the 'new Jerusalem' in a 'new heaven' and 'new earth'.

All these excellent scholars discuss typology from an historical perspective, and tend to concentrate on a 'local' typology, whether medieval, Renaissance, early American or Victorian. They are all interested in how typology is *applied* by literature, art or history-writing. Since Erich Auerbach's classic essay on 'Figura' (1938) the most significant theoretical and critical investigation into the nature of typology has been made by Northrop Frye. Therefore it is time to turn to his ideas.

NORTHROP FRYE AND THE REDISCOVERY OF TYPOLOGY

One professional biblical scholar wrote of Northrop Frye that he 'in a paragraph can throw more light on the Christian Bible than one usually finds in several issues of technical journals.'[5] Frye himself admitted that 'all my critical work has revolved around the Bible.'[6] We might even risk the statement that all his writings on the Bible have revolved around typology. Indeed, an unceasing interest in typology seems to be a *leitmotif* in his academic career. But this tentative statement needs substantiation.

From Frye's recent biography we learn how much, as both a student of Blake and of theology, Frye resisted the prevailing historical trend in biblical studies. Blake's understanding of the unity of the Bible was antithetical to the rationalistic, historical analysis which hindered scholars from a symbolical reading and recreation of the text. Therefore instead of being distracted by the huge quantity of technical scholarship on the Bible, Frye turned to St Augustine's typological treatise, *The City of God* and to the writings of Hugh of St. Victor, which conceived the cathedral and even the world as a 'book'. He was fascinated by Emile Mâle's volumes describing the iconography of typological windows in French cathedrals.[7]

At the beginning of *The Great Code* Frye writes as follows:

> the analytical and historical approach that has dominated Biblical criticism for over a century was of relatively little use to me . . . At no point does it throw light on how or why a poet might read the Bible . . . There remained the more traditional

approaches of medieval typology and of certain forms of Reformation commentary. They were more congenial to me because they accepted the unity of the Bible as postulate.[8]

Moving away from biographical considerations which support the thesis that typology has long been a central concern with Frye, we should look at how it has been present – latently at first – in his major works becoming manifest as a central subject matter and structural principle in *The Great Code*.

It has been mentioned that Frye's interest in typology comes from his study of Blake, *Fearful Symmetry* (1947). Blake conceived of the Bible as an imaginative unity against the then new rationalistic tendencies that prised apart the various layers of Scripture. Blake's art can be understood as a case against Locke and as a conscious preference for an alternative tradition epitomized by the symbolical universe of Swedenborg. Frye also recognized that typology is a central aspect of Milton's poetry and in 1956 he published an essay on 'Typology in Milton's *Paradise Regained*' that was later incorporated into his book on Milton, *The Return of Eden* (1965). Typology is not yet an explicit principle in his rightly celebrated *Anatomy of Criticism* (1957) but nevertheless it is present latently, throughout the whole work. Frye laments in the introduction that 'Biblical typology is so dead a language now that most readers, including scholars, cannot construe the superficial meaning of any poem which employs it'.[9] In the *Anatomy* typology is applied as a 'heuristic principle' of a genuine higher criticism of the Bible that perceives the 'synthesizing process' and the imaginative unity of the Bible. When writing about 'Specific Encyclopedic Forms' Frye wittily dethrones the historical-analytical tradition from its self-proclaimed status of 'higher criticism' and by reversing its place in the hierarchy of studies he calls it, in fact, 'straw-thrashing' *lower* criticism, which sees in the biblical texts only corruptions, glosses, redactions, insertions, conflations or misunderstandings. For him the 'genuine' higher criticism of the Bible is a purely literary criticism that conceives the typological unity which was constructed by all those redactions or insertions that the historical critics are so keen on finding. He writes:

> A genuine higher criticism of the Bible, therefore, would be a synthesizing process which would start with the assumption that the Bible is a definite myth, a single archetypal structure

extending from creation to apocalypse. Its heuristic principle would be St Augustine's axiom that the Old Testament is revealed in the New and the New is concealed in the Old: that the two testaments are not so much allegories of one another as metaphorical identifications of one another. We cannot trace the Bible back, even historically, to a time when its materials were not being shaped into a typological unity, and if the Bible is to be regarded as inspired in any sense, sacred or secular, its editorial and redacting processes must be regarded as inspired too.[10]

Frye uses the term 'myth' in its original, Aristotelian sense: *mythos*, meaning 'story'. In his 'Theory of Myth' Frye mentions that there are two concentric quest-myths in the Bible: the Genesis-apocalypse myth and the Exodus-millenium myth. These concentric quest-myths are typologically related to one-another:

> In the former Adam is cast out of Eden, loses the river of life and the tree of life, and wanders in the labyrinth of human history until he is restored to his original state by the Messiah. In the latter Israel is cast out of its inheritance and wanders in the labyrinth of Egyptian and Babylonian captivity until he is restored to his original state in the Promised Land. Eden and the Promised Land, therefore, are typologically identical, as are the tyrannies of Egypt and Babylon and the wilderness of the law.[11]

Frye adds at this point that a literary or cultural critic can only deal with the Bible in this way 'as a major informing influence on literary symbolism.'

Frye's earlier and undeclared gravitation towards typology comes to full manifestation in *The Great Code* (1982). Typology has now become both a central subject-matter and also a structural principle of *The Great Code* itself. Out of eight chapters two bear the title of typology. Part One ('The Order of Words'), discussing language, metaphor and myth, concludes with typology and Part Two ('The Order of Types') begins with typology and reverses the order.

Frye mentions that in the Bible the 'two testaments form a double mirror, each reflecting the other but neither the world outside.'[12] We have to emphasize here that *The Great Code* itself is structured as a 'double-mirror': Part One ('The Order of Words: Language I,

Metaphor I, Myth I, Typology I') is *recreated* by Part Two ('The Order of Types: Typology II, Myth II, Metaphor II, Language II'). Thus Part One is the 'type' in *The Great Code*, and it is 'fulfilled' by Part Two, which is the 'antitype'. Moreover, the whole of *The Great Code* is the 'antitype', or, *recreation*, of the Bible. It means that Frye does not write about the Bible by explaining it, but comments upon it by *recreating* it. Once again, in Frye's hands, the subject-matter has been converted into art. The reader, as he once remarked in connection with Shakespeare, is not invited to 'admire' the art (and especially not the artist!) but the end of such a study is to 'possess' this art so that the verbal energy may filter into his mind and shape his power of thinking.

Frye has introduced at least two significant theoretical innovations concerned with typology, besides his own application of typology as a way of writing about the Bible. His first significant and genuine insight concerns typology as a figure of speech. If we compare typology with metaphor, we can see that while the latter is a simultaneous figure of speech, typology is 'a figure that moves in time: the type exists in the past and the antitype in the present or the type exists in the present and the antitype in the future.'[13] Having read Kierkegaard's book *Repetition*, Frye observed that there are only two figures that move in time: 'causality' and 'typology'. But while the former rhetorical form is a backward-looking, past-oriented one and is based on reason, observation and knowledge, typology is a forward-looking, future-oriented figure based on faith, hope and vision.

At the beginning of his book Frye differentiated between three phases of language: (a) the metaphorical-poetic, 'this is that' phase; (b) the metonymic-dialectical 'this is for that' phase; and (c) the descriptive-demotic phase. We shall soon come back to the problem of biblical, 'kerygmatic' language, which, according to Frye, originates in the first metaphorical phase of language though 'much of the Bible is contemporary with the second phase separation of the dialectical from the poetic.'[14] It is important for us to evoke this threefold distinction because it is the only way to understand that typology comes closest to the metaphorical or poetic phase. Frye calls this form of expression *kerygma* or the language of proclamation.[15] Causality, however, is a later product. It is somewhere between the second and the third phases of language. Having all this in mind it should not be difficult to understand why Frye is so dissatisfied with the historical criticism of the Bible. He finds that the historical-critical discourse is not adequate for biblical interpretation. Why? Because the historical-critical discourse is *causal* discourse and the main body of the Bible is that of an anti-causal or typological discourse which demands its own way of speaking, commentary or hermeneutics. Instead of imposing our own historical preconceptions *on* the Bible we have to subordinate ourselves to the discourse *of* the Bible. As Paul Ricoeur says in his new, 'intratextual' theory of the text: 'interpretation is not an act *on* the text, but an act *of* the text.'[16] It is remarkable that the postmodern idea of 'intertextuality' bears a conspicuous resemblance to the Reformation principle of *scriptura sacra sui ipsius interpres* (the Holy Scripture interprets itself).

Frye's second new insight is his heuristic distinction between the 'phases of revelation'. He distinguishes seven 'phases': creation, revolution (exodus), Law, wisdom, prophecy, gospel, and apocalypse. He interprets them as 'each phase being the type of the one following it and the antitype of the one preceding it.'[17] He observes the 'progress' of the antitypes, which, he finds, is a progress of intensification in which newer perpectives are continually being opened up until this progress arrives at apocalypse, which means revelation. 'At the end of the Book of Revelation, with such phrases as 'I make all things new' (21:5) and the promise of a new heaven and earth, we reach the antitype of all antitypes, the real beginning of light and sound of which the first word of the Bible is the type.'[18]

It follows from this that typology ends in a theory of history, what the Germans called *Heilsgeschichte* (translated into English variously as 'sacred history', 'salvation history' or 'redemptive history'). True, this originally biblical notion of history was converted into the secular idea of 'progress' sometime in the eighteenth century. It was adopted by the enthusiastic progress-believers in the eighteenth and the nineteenth centuries as a 'one-directional and irreversible conception of history.'[19] This secular vision, it seems to me, is a parody of the originally sacred vision of history. Perhaps the indifference, ignorance and unpopularity of typology today can be explained by the fact that the ideas of Marx, and all the optimistic secular eschatologies have proved to be failures in any practical sense. But simply because the vision, parodied, fails, it does not follow that the vision itself is doomed.

Finally, it should be said that Frye's innovative understanding of typology argues strongly for the inner coherence and the imaginative unity of the Bible. In his vision, typology 'particularly in its spiralling phases, gives the Bible thematic unity, the recurring imagery furnishes a protracted motival unity.'[20] This imaginative unity becomes evident in stylistic characteristics, especially in the repetitive symmetry of the narrative: one who would understand the New Testament, first should understand the Old Testament.[21]

Unfortunately theologians very rarely seem to have benefited from Frye's critical insights. Two names, however, break the mould. The Canadian Catholic theologian, Joseph P. Cahill has published a number of articles in which he recognizes the theological significance of Frye's literary criticism. He writes:

> the outcome of literary criticism is not to uncover external decoration or ornamentary form . . . but to disclose that the theological and religious meaning in the Bible is inextricably bound up with its literary character.[22]

The other theologian whose work bears a conspicuous resemblance to that of Frye is the Protestant scholar from Yale, the founder of 'canonical criticism', Brevard S. Childs. Though I cannot find any direct connection between Frye and Childs, the convergence of their thought is more than remarkable. Childs criticized efforts to locate the 'literal sense' and the 'original meaning' of Scripture 'behind' the text, in a historical reality because in practice this leads to the loss of the idea of 'scope' and the 'shape' of Scripture brought about by the community of faith.[23] For Childs the true 'context' of Scripture is the 'canon' and not the historical reality behind it. Childs' programme of 'relocating' the literal sense of Scripture in the canon is very similar to Frye's typological vision of Scripture which highlights its unique, imaginative unity, its 'artistic' shape. Gerald T. Sheppard has also noted the similar concerns of Frye as a literary critic and Childs as a biblical scholar. Frye conceives the Bible as an imaginative unity, Childs sees it as 'Scripture'. But while Frye presents his insights on the grounds of language, Childs and Sheppard argue for the 'shape' of the Bible on historical-critical grounds. Sheppard, for example is interested in 'canon-conscious redactions' and therefore he concentrates 'on the indications within the text of how editors in the late stages of the formation of biblical books registered their assumptions that these books belong together within a common intertext of Scripture.'[24]

THE RISK OF TYPOLOGY

As I said in the beginning, I am inviting the reader into a forgotten no man's land. Once upon a time it was a well-cultivated, perhaps even overcultivated land. We can say that it had two 'golden ages': the first in Patristic Christianity and the second in seventeenth century Protestantism. It may be significant that of the scholars who have turned to typology from a historical point of view, several appear to come from the extreme opposites of the Christian tradition: we find among them scholars with a Jesuit as well as with a radical Protestant background. But their purpose is not that of a genuine critical estimation of typology but mainly a historical or archeological reconstruction. The work of the critic, however, is undoubtedly risky, particularly if he or she chooses to argue against the popular current of opinion. I believe that criticism has always had a prophetic role: the critic of conviction is constrained to voice his or her opinion. And a true critic can never be a flatterer.

We have said that typology is a forgotten language, but why is this? The history of thought may provide us with a possible answer. The idea of progress, the optimistic belief in the increase of knowledge, the belief in the development of society, the improvement of humanity has been with us since the Enlightenment. This noble thought has had some concomitant defects since the beginning of its career but we became aware of it only in our century. This thinking, so keen to acknowledge the significance of the 'new' and the 'unknown', has failed to recognize a law – namely, that every gain entails a certain loss. The 'principle of development' could prosper only by suppressing the 'principle of remembrance'. The rationalistic, discursive thinking based on 'clear and distinct' ideas has prompted us to look only ahead, to investigate only the unknown because it was assumed to be the only way to progress. As a result, the 'symbolical consciousness' faded and only some isolated rebels – like Blake, Kierkegaard and Nietzsche – have protested against the dominance of exclusively rationalistic thinking. The result of this tendency has been the 'waste-land experience' of our century beginning with crisis and war instead of 'the promised end'. Several thinkers, seeking causes for these crises, have given up optimistic beliefs. Poets like Eliot, philosophers like Gadamer have turned to what they have called 'tradition'. And they have found something: a forgotten, symbolical consciousness which has relevance, or even a message, for today. The symbol carries an archaic, hidden meaning for the future. The symbol was born frequently under persecution or in suffering. Therefore it had to hide itself. But its power is derived very much from its hiddenness. The symbol both covers and manifests, it both conceals and reveals. The symbol provokes interpretation, as Paul Ricoeur says: 'the symbol gives rise to thought.'[25] Typology as symbolism of a special kind has also been dismissed, forgotten or neglected. But it still exists, it still calls for interpretation, it claims attention far beyond an antiquarian interest. It remains a living linguistic principle that we use day by day and live by. Its critical revival is unavoidable.

However, typology is risky not only because it is for many a forgotten grammar. It is even more risky because it is an extremely sensitive issue among those who have not not forgotten about it. There are two antagonistic groups who passionately resist typology. Evoking a famous passage by St Paul, we might say that for the first group typology is 'scandal' and for the second one it is 'foolishness'. From the first group we hear the passionate protest of a Harold Bloom:

> The Old Testament is far too strong a poetry to be fulfilled by its revisionary descendent, the self-proclaimed New Testament . . . We may wonder whether the idea of figura was ever more than a self-deception . . . I am an enemy of the New Testament. My enmity is lifelong, and intensifies as I study its text more closely . . . Frye's code, like Erich Auerbach's *figura*, . . . is only another belated repetition of the Christian appropriation and usurpation of the Hebrew Bible . . .[26]

While Bloom and others consider typology as a means of 'usurpation' of the strong text of the Hebrew Bible, there is another group for whom typology is not 'scandal' but rather 'foolishness'. A knowledgeable theologian wrote in the first half of this century:

> typology has always flourished in times of ignorance and decay of learning.[27]

While the first group rejects typology on behalf of the Old Testament, this second group dismisses it on behalf of the New Testament. Marcion rejected the Old Testament in the second century, and certainly, this Marcionite tendency is detectable in some twentieth century German theology. Some critics of this tendency relate an occasional Marcionite attitude toward the Old Testament to a distortion of the law and gospel dialectic in Lutheranism. One can recall the practice of the 1930s in Nazi Germany when some Germans, in their ambition to eliminate Judaism from Christianity, encouraged the compilation of a 'Nazi-Bible' that would dismiss the Old Testament from the canon and replace it by Teutonic mythology. This was, of course, an extreme case, and therefore one cannot but appreciate that the only comprehensive and standard monograph on typology, Leonard Goppelt's *Typos*, was written in such a climate in 1939.[28] Bultmann's attack on Goppelt and typology in 1950[29] is, of course, far from such low sentiments, but one is not certain whether his theology is absolutely free from a Marcionite attitude.

Typology, we have seen, is risky. It is unknown to the majority of people. For a certain minority it is scandal, for another group it is foolishness. Prejudice, whether anti-semitic or anti-Christian, might be a great obstacle in understanding or accepting typology. In the following pages I am not going to advocate an uncritical embracing of typology. A historical survey of biblical interpretation could show many fanciful and even shocking examples of typology. But an abuse of a principle should never annihilate the principle itself. I am convinced that typology is a principle inherent in biblical language. Therefore it seems advisable to begin my discussion with the problem of language.

2
The Hermeneutical Context

My purpose in this Chapter is to shed some new light on typology. To do this, I have chosen to discuss typology hermeneutically rather than historically. What is the difference between a 'hermeneutical' and a 'historical' approach? To put it very briefly we may say that for a hermeneutical approach the primary reality is language and not history, as language rather than history is the 'home of meaning'. In the following threefold division of the 'hermeneutics of typology' I am following a threefold division of hermeneutics invented by some eighteenth-century German Pietists. For them the three phases of hermeneutics were: (1) *ars intelligendi* (the art of understanding); (2) *ars explicandi* (the art of explanation); (3) *ars applicandi* (the art of application). Thus the section on language may correspond to 'understanding'; the section on meaning to 'explanation'; and the section on reading to 'application'. There is, however, an organic interrelationship between these phases as if they merged into one another and therefore any arbitrary separation of one phase from other would do violent damage to the hermeneutic texture.

LANGUAGE: FROM FIGURE TO FULFILMENT

We have seen already that typology, contrary to the opinions of its frequent misinterpreters and misusers, is not a doctrinal issue, but is rooted in, and has much to do with, the *language* of the Bible. It is more closely bound up with the metaphorical-poetic, 'this is that' phase of language. If typology originates in, and is bound up with, this biblical language, then we must have a closer look at the special nature and dynamics of this language. Wherein lies the speciality of biblical language? Sometimes people say that it is 'performative' rather than 'informative'; some others claim that it is 'figurative' rather than 'literal'. Sometimes it is said that it is 'symbolic', 'emotive' rather than 'referential', that it is 'connotative', 'associative', rather than 'denotative'. Finally, some others maintain that it is the 'language of persuasion' rather than the 'language of statements'. But these pairs of contrasts mark the difference between the language of science and the language of literature. Our question is: is biblical language exactly the same as literary language? Or can we perhaps specify more exactly what we mean by 'biblical language'?

It is not my purpose to argue that biblical language is exactly the same as poetic language, for the Bible is not just a 'poem'. To elucidate the specific nature of biblical language I shall look at two terms, one used by Northrop Frye, the other by Paul Ricoeur.

Northrop Frye borrowed Rudolf Bultmann's phrase (but not his meaning!) when he emphasized that biblical language is the language of *kerygma*, that is, the language of 'proclamation'. Each language of proclamation is, by its nature, a rhetorical language which uses figures of speech but *kerygma* is a special kind of rhetoric:

> *Kerygma* is a mode of rhetoric, though it is rhetoric of a special kind. It is, like all rhetoric, a mixture of the metaphorical and the 'existential' or concerned but, unlike practically all other forms of rhetoric, it is not an argument disguised by figuration . . . the word *kerygma* is associated with the theology of Bultmann, and in Bultmann's view *kerygma* is to be opposed to myth, which he regards as an obstacle to it . . . [but] . . . myth is the linguistic vehicle of *kerygma*, and that to 'demythologize' any part of the Bible would be the same as to obliterate it.[1]

We can perhaps add that the rhetoric of proclamation is not to be understood as the writer's own rhetoric – it is far beyond it, and, in any case, it is within the text, it is carried by the text. The figures of metaphorical language are not ornaments of thought or 'beautiful expressions of some high theological ideas'. Twentieth century views of language resist such dualistic or 'expressive' or referential notions: language is not simply the 'means' of expression but frequently 'the thing itself'. When Frye says that the language of proclamation is the 'vehicle of revelation' he does not have the descriptive, referential or populist view in mind. Against such simplistic views he believes that the Bible is too deeply rooted in all resources of language[2] and therefore the language of proclamation is the language of power. Indeed, the Bible radiates power by means of words,³ and the purpose of its rhetoric is to affect, transform and change its reader. Instead of conveying a 'literal truth', as the populists believe, this language has an exclusive claim for truth in its own terms as it definitely aims to demolish and overcome its readers' sense of reality. Auerbach convincingly illustrated this aspect of biblical language in his opening essay of the *Mimesis* on 'Odysseus' Scar':

> The Scripture stories do not, like Homer's court out of favour, that they may please us and enchant us – they seek to subject us, and if we refuse to be subjected, we are rebels.⁴

Proclamation. persuasion, power: these are indeed important marks of biblical language but in our search for the nature of this language we have not yet arrived at the heart of the problem. The power of the 'Word', the 'double-edged sword' is, above all, *a creative* power. I do not propose that the words have power in themselves, as this notion would assume magic; this creative power is attributed to their divine provenance: they are sent out by the power of God. Thus the word is able to reach its readers again and again, after more than a thousand years, and, as Isaiah says, it never remains 'void', it 'prospers in the thing it was sent to'. However, biblical language does not simply create readers, but it is also able to *recreate* itself. We shall see that reading and interpretation is also a 'rewriting, or recreating, of the text. Frye writes: 'Every reader recreates what he reads... Recreation of this sort always involves some kind of translation.'⁵ Here Northrop Frye's programme exactly coincides with that of Paul Ricoeur, who, in his *Symbolism of Evil* writes:

> It is not regret for the sunken Atlantides that animates us, but *hope for* a *re-creation of language*. Beyond the desert of criticism, we wish to be called again.⁶

So far we have seen that biblical language is a proclamative, persuasive, powerful, creative and recreative language. In order to make a further step towards typology we have to apply here a remark on symbolical language by Paul Ricoeur. Ricoeur speaks about the 'fullness of language'. 'The fullness consists in the fact that the second meaning somehow dwells on the first meaning.'⁷ Ricoeur confesses that his interest in *full* language and *bound* language is subjective because 'my meaning' (the second meaning) dwells in the other (the first meaning):

> How does that which binds meaning to meaning bind me? The movement that draws me toward the second meaning assimilates me to what is said, makes me participate in what is announced to me . . . it is an existential assimilation . . . of my being to being.[8]

Applying Ricoeur's insights to our subject of inquiry, that is to biblical language, we might perhaps say that biblical language is *fulfilment-language*. Its provocative, enigmatic nature yearns for a stillness. It is resolved, 'satisfied', if it comes to a fullness, if it is 'fulfilled'.

My aim is a new, fresh understanding of typology. We have seen that it was an issue of biblical language and therefore we had to approach the nature of biblical language. But before coming to a new understanding of typology we have to anatomize two words in our title, 'figure' and 'fulfill'. My final aim is to define these words in terms of each other; and it is our hope that by illuminating this mutual dynamic we shall be able to gain some new insights.

Anatomy of the Noun 'Figure'

I do not wish to recapitulate what Erich Auerbach has written about the classical and biblical origins of the word 'Figura' in his scholarly essay. We shall return to the theoretical conclusions of Auerbach's historical and philological investigations when we try to set our two anatomized words into motion by defining their mutual interrelationship. Here we shall confine our anatomy to the Greek origins of the word as it crops up in the New Testament; its cognates, the word denoting 'pattern' and eventually its synonymms.

Figura is the Latin translation of the Greek *typos* which means 'pattern', 'example', 'model' 'mould'. This noun is derived from the verb *typtein* which means 'to strike' or 'to stupefy by a blow', 'to stamp on a mark', 'to impress a figure'. *Typos* may denote also 'scar', 'print of nails' (John 20:25). It may also refer to the 'example of obedience of faith', a 'model' to be imitated by the

Christian. St Paul uses the word in such a sense several times (for example, 1 Thessalonians 1:7; 2 Thessalonians 3:9; Philippians 3:17 etc.). Leonard Goppelt, the author of the still standard monograph on *Typos* (1939) writes: 'The more a life is moulded by the word, the more it becomes *typos*, a model, or mould.'[9] In Romans 6:17 the teaching is called a *typos*, a 'mould', into which the Christian is placed to be formed by God. *Typos* in two New Testament passages refers to the 'heavenly original'. Both Acts 7:44 and Hebrews 8:5 are understood as references to Exodus 25:40 where the 'heavenly original' is rendered by the Septuagint as *typos*. In the Epistle to the Hebrews typology has a special significance: here *typos* appears rather in a 'vertical' sense, while in all other cases it is seen 'horizontally'. The 'fulfilment' of *typos* is the *antitypos*. The latter word is used only twice in the New Testament, in Hebrews 9:24 and 1 Peter 3:21.

The most significant application of the word is by St Paul, who uses the word as a hermeneutical term. In the classical passage of 1 Corinthians 10 St Paul describes some events of the Old Testament as *typoi* in order to show that those events point to the significant events in the present stage of salvation history. Paul refers to the Exodus experience of ancient Israel at the Red Sea and their wanderings in the desert. He recalls these Old Testament events in retrospect, now having the Christian sacraments: baptism and the eucharist in mind. The fathers were baptised 'unto Moses' while they 'passed through the sea'; and they ate the 'spiritual food' and drank the 'spiritual drink' and they were followed by the 'spiritual Rock', 'and that Rock was Christ'. Those Old Testament events are seen as examples that are evoked to warn those, who, in the present (and higher) stage of salvation history are meant to be the people of God. They are admonished not to fall into the same type of mistake, not to abuse God's grace again.

> Now these things were our *examples* (*typoi*), to the intent we should not lust after evil things . . .   (10:6)
> Now all these things happened to them for *ensamples* (*typikos*): and they are written for our admonition, upon whom the ends of the world are come.   (10:11)

St Paul's most famous application of *typos* as a hermeneutical term is in Romans 5:14:

Nevertheless death reigned from Adam to Moses, even them that had not sinned after the similitude of Adam's transgression, who is the *figure* of him that was to come (*typos tou mellonthos*).

There is an antithetical correspondance between Adam, whose act of disobedience brought death to mankind, and Christ's act of obedience that regained salvation for human kind. *Typos* can be used also in an antithetical construction. Adam, the 'old' man is not 'finished', nor 'perfect'; his fall created a vacuum that is 'filled in' by Christ. Christ as the antitype is the fulfilment of the 'hollow mould' of Adam, and thus Christ perfects the fatally injured status of man – he is *the* man.

Is *typos* the only word to denote 'pattern' or 'model' in the New Testament? Of course, not. For example, when the apostle mentions Sodom and Gomorrah as warning examples of divine retribution, he uses the word *deigma* (Jude 7) or *hypodeigma* (2 Peter 2:6). The word *hypodeigma* is used several times, not only in the sense of an example but also in the sense of suggestion (Hebrews 8:5; 9:23). This word is used also in James 5:10 where the apostle encourages his fellow Christians to take the prophets as *hypodeigma*. In John's Gospel it is used in connection with the washing of the disciples feet (13:15). *Hypotyposis*, a cognate of *typos* meaning 'outline to be filled in', is used twice, in both cases by St Paul. In 1 Timothy 1:16 Christ, it is suggested, left the apostle an 'example' while in 2 Timothy 1:13 St Paul claims that he has given Timothy the 'outline' or 'pattern' of sound teaching. We find the word *hypogrammos* in 1 Peter 2:21 where Christ is seen to have left an example that we should follow his steps. Furthermore, the *parabole* is also used in the sense of *typos* in Hebrews 9:9 just as the word *allegorumena* in Galatians 4:24. The latter word refers to the two sons of Abraham: Ishmael and Isaac who are said to have 'exemplified' the two covenants: the covenant of law and the covenant of promise. Here Paul uses the word not in the 'Greek', philosophical sense but rather in the 'Hebraic' sense of the parable. That is the reason why the representatives of the School of Antioch (fourth century) who were desperately fighting against the allegorizing tendencies of the School of Alexandria (Clement, Origen and so on) were so keen on commenting on this passage in Galatians, where they emphasized that St Paul had used the word 'allegory' only formally but what he had actually meant was 'theoria', as they called it.

So far we have mainly been concerned with the anatomy of the word 'figure' in the sense of 'outline' or 'pattern'. There is, however, a word that more precisely reflects the dynamics inherent in *typos* or *figura*. The word 'shadow' (*skia*) is used in the New Testament when St Paul and the author of the Epistle to the Hebrews speak about the relationship of the 'old' and the 'new', the 'law' and the 'gospel'.

St Paul writes in Colossians 2:16–17 as follows:

> Let no man therefore judge you in meat, or in drink, or in respect of an holyday, or of the new moon, or of the sabbath days: *which are* a shadow *of things to come* (*skia ton mellonton*), but the body is of Christ.

Similar is the structure of Romans 5:14 where Adam was a 'figure of him that was to come'. Here the Jewish feasts are seen as 'a shadow of things to come'. The other example is from Hebrews 10:1:

> For the law, having a *shadow of things to come* and not the very image of the things, can never with those sacrifices which they offered year by year continually to make the comers thereunto perfect.

Without going into exegetical details I intend to concentrate on the power of this metaphor which often has fascinated the imagination of artists. Milton, for one, adopted this metaphor in his *Paradise Lost*: 'From Shadowy Types to Truth, from Flesh to Spirit' (XII, l. 303).[10]

The interplay of 'shadow' and 'substance' is not a peculiar feature of the Bible as it goes back to the platonic understanding of reality (to the famous cave-simile in the *Republic*) but the way it is presented in the Bible is radically different from the conventional platonic sense. Plato and his followers use it in a spatial-vertical sense (shadow: 'down' – true reality: 'up'), while in the Bible it appears in a temporal-horizontal sense: (shadow: 'old' – reality: 'new'). The Bible radically affirms the reality of time and temporal movement and thus it perceives the world in terms of past, present and future; it radically affirms the beginning and the end against the cyclical views of paganism. It follows from this view that the past has its meaning for the present. Therefore, unlike the platonic view of the universe, the 'shadow' is not identical with an insubstantial meaninglessness. The 'shadow' or the past is also relevant on its own terms, partly because it serves as an 'example'for the present; partly – and more importantly – the shadows or figures are seen as *inseparable* from their fulfilments: the past is pregnant with the future; it carries the germs of things to come just as the seed is the plant in potential. I would hope to make it increasingly obvious that behind the biblical shadow-substance (body) metaphor there is a strong philosophy of history. The biblical shadow-substance metaphor maintains a constant gaze for the future and it implies that the present yearns for completion.

The Latin translation of *skia* is *umbra* and it has been used synonymously with *figura*, the Latin translation of *typos*. The Church-Fathers began to use the verbalized forms of these nouns: *prefigurare* or *adumbrare*. These verbs have passed into English without difficulty: 'prefigure' or 'adumbrate' are the same as 'foreshadow'. But before passing on to the discussion of the power of verbs let us conclude our anatomy of nouns with the following chart:

PAST (or Present)		PRESENT (or Future)
typos		*antitypos*
figura		*substantia*
	prefigurare	
skia		*aletheia*
umbra		*veritas*
(shadow)	*adumbrare*	(truth)

Anatomy of the Verb 'Fulfil'

The first part of our anatomy was devoted to nouns. At the end we saw that these nouns have gradually been given a verbal force and the Church-Fathers have begun to coin verbs out of nouns. Nouns are necessary for our grasping the objects we perceive around us in the world. But nouns come and go, they appear and fade away, they are born and die. More precisely: we bring them to the world and we bury them when we do not find them useful any more. Such is probably the case with the noun 'God'. Since Nietzsche's statement 'God is dead', the traditional views of God have radically been challenged. But Northrop Frye reminds us that this may be only a statement about the limitations of our language, especially of its descriptive phase. He accepts that God as a 'noun' might be dead, because our use of his name was perhaps a mere fallacy. But if we consider the burning bush story where God's self-revelation – 'I am who I am' – can also be translated 'I will be what I will be', then we might perhaps be able to grasp something from the mystery of that God, namely that God is a 'verb' rather than a noun, and as such (it) *is*. God is 'not simply as a verb of asserted existence but a verb expressing a process *fulfilling itself*.'[11] This thrilling perception also encourages us to move on from the anatomy of the noun 'figure' towards the anatomy of a verb, especially when this verb happens to be: 'fulfil'.

The verbs 'fill up', 'fulfil' or 'complete' are used in the New Testament with conspicuous frequency. We often read that prophecies are fulfilled, 'time is fulfilled' (Mark 1:15); 'the law is fulfilled', 'the Scripture is fulfilled' and we hear time and again that things happen 'so that it might be fulfilled'. As it has been said to before, biblical language is indeed 'fulfilment language'.

We should notice that this fulfilment language is used even in the negative sense. Jesus chides the religious authorities:

> Fill ye up then the measure of your fathers.   (Matthew 23: 32)

St Paul writes that the Jews by disobeying the Gospel 'fill up their sin' (1 Thessalonians 2:16). The recurring formula 'that it might be fulfilled' is most frequently used by Matthew (1:22; 2:15; 2:23; 4:14; 8:17; 12:17; 13:35; 21:4; 26:56) but it also turns up in John (19:24; 19:28; 19:36). Indeed, one might gain the uncomfortable impression that everything had to take place out of necessity as if it had been prescribed in a divine scenario. Imagine what a historically-minded newcomer to the New Testament might say when he reads that one of the last words of the agonized Christ – 'I am thirsty' – was uttered only 'so that the Scripture might be fulfilled' (John 19:28). This construction, in fact, suggests that the plan or the design had already been written by God and yet it had to be carried out by the free will of Christ. C. F. D. Moule writes:

> the phrase 'all this took place to fulfil' bears witness to the paradox that the Incarnation is the meeting place of free will and predestination. That 'the Son of Man must suffer' is not contradicted but rather complemented, by the declaration 'I lay down my life . . . of my own accord'.   (John 10: 17–18)[12]

So one central (and paradoxical) notion in Jesus' ministry is that he has to fulfil God's will by his own free will. It is a *leitmotif* in the New Testament that the Old Testament law is fulfilled in Christ: 'I am not come to destroy but to fulfil' (Matthew 5:17) or, 'the love is the fulfilling of the law' (Romans 13:10).

From these examples we can infer that the biblical use and operation of 'fulfilment' is far more complex than a simplistic and mechanical 'prediction-fulfilment' model would suggest. The biblical idea of fulfilment is organically bound up with biblical language. As Brevard Childs has convincingly argued, the biblical sense of 'fulfilment' does not involve the idea of identical correspondances or the matching of two independent entities:

> It is non-Hebraic thinking which tries to relate prophecy and fulfilment in terms of exactness of correspondence based on a Greek theory of truth. The Hebrew view of fulfilment does not consider them as two independent entities whose relation is determined by an external criterion.[13]

Fulfilment in the Bible is the 'filling in' of the 'word'. The true word is the one which is filled, it comes to life when it reaches its destination, when the reader or the hearer of the word resonates to its power just as a lamp is lit when it is connected to an electric circuit. God's word, we read in Isaiah, never returns void as it is destined to accomplish its task (55:11). God fulfils 'with his hands' he spoke with his mouth (2 Chronicles 6:4). According to Childs:

> The word maintains itself by reaching the wholeness of God's purpose for it. The true word possesses an independent existence since it is part of the totality towards which it moves. If it is a filled word, it also shares in that reality. It hastens towards its end and cannot be stopped (c.f. Hab. 2:3) . . . The true word continues until it forms a totality with that reality of which it is already a part. Word and sign have much in common since they both point toward a totality while already possessing a portion of the anticipated reality. A word is fulfilled when it is filled full to form a whole.[14]

We can learn more about 'fulfilment' if we proceed to define it in terms of 'figure' and then to define 'figure' in terms of 'fulfilment'. This issue will be taken up also in the discussion of 'Meaning', (especially in the section on 'fuller meaning'); and we shall also relate it to the problem of 'Reading' at the end of this Chapter.

Figure and Fulfilment – Toward a new Understanding of Typology

I am proposing to understand 'figure' with the help of 'fulfilment' and 'fulfilment' with the help of 'figure'. In attempting such an 'interdefinition' I shall apply Paul Ricoeur's structure of logic implied in his definition of symbol and interpretation. Ricoeur says that the symbol is a 'double-meaning linguistic expression that requires an interpretation' and interpretation is a 'work of understanding that aims at deciphering symbols'.[15] In a similar way I am suggesting a stipulative definition. Accordingly, the *figure* ('*type*' or '*shadow*') is a *linguistic* expression that requires fulfilment. *Fulfilment*, on the other hand is the '*filling in*' of the *incompleteness*, '*voidness*', or '*emptiness*' created by the power of the figure.

We must here recall that *typos* goes back to *typtein* which means 'to strike'. The blow or the striking resulted in a voidness or emptiness as an imprint is left when a comet hits the surface of the earth. This hole or vacuum is an enigma or a question, which requires, or even provokes fulfilment. The biblical text is frequently marked by such 'holes' (some would say divine fingerprints) that yearn for completion and fulfilment. The type, unlike the symbol, is originally concrete and historical (as a person, event or 'thing') but these concrete historical entities carry a *surplus of meaning*, they are more than what they historically are, the type is 'pregnant' with a ✓ future meaning. It implies that these historical entities *as* historical entities are perfect in themselves but this inherent 'surplus' in them calls for greater perfection or completion. The figure is like a seed that has yet to grow. The term 'figure fulfilled' goes back to Tertullian who frequently used the expression '*figuram* implere'. It means that whoever fulfils the figure identifies himself not simply with that historical figure but with the surplus of meaning inherent in that figure. The expression 'to fulfil a figure' is only a variant of the New Testament expression 'the Scripture fulfilled': *peplerotai he graphe* (Luke 4:21, cf. Mark 15:28). What is the meaning of this frequently mentioned but often misunderstood expression? It involves the notion that Scripture, (and we can say the same of 'figure' or of 'law'), was powerless or 'empty' in itself but by the new eschatological event it is again 'filled up' like an accumulator so that the word is once again at work, it is able to radiate anew its creative power.

The type, just like the metaphor, is a statement of identity. But we shall soon see that the type differs from the metaphor as it immediately evokes the background of salvation history: the identification with biblical figures tends to be more provocative than the identification with a fictional or a historical figure. You deepen your understanding of a person if you say 'You are Electra' or 'You are Hamlet' but there is probably an eschatological touch in saying that 'You are Moses' or 'You are Elijah'. For somebody in the Christian community it is probably more chilling and frightening to hear that 'You are Judas' than 'You are Hitler', as the despair of Judas has traditionally been associated with damnation.

The Bible, as we have said, manifests salvation history with the presupposition that time 'grows'. The biblical figures, we have also seen, carry this surplus of meaning and this 'surplus' is also growing. It is not possible to fulfil the figures at any time; they can be fulfilled only when time is 'ripe'. Therefore one can fulfil a figure only if one also fulfils the time. There were many Pseudo-Messiahs yet it was only Christ who began his ministry by announcing 'Time is fulfilled' (*peplerotai ho kairos*; Mark 1:15), and his redemptive activity took place in the 'fullness of time' (*to pleroma tu khronu*; Galatians 4:4). Fulfilment is the identifion of oneself with that surplus of the figure in the right time. Only Christ could fulfil the figure of Adam, only the Gospel could fulfil the Law, only the Eucharist could fulfil the Passover. When fulfilling the figure in the right time, the antitype, becomes the *forma perfectior*, it means that an eschatological event takes place: the creation is perfected.

What is the relationship between interpretation and fulfilment? Each fulfilment, we can say, is interpretation but each interpretation is not necessarily fulfilment. To interpret something means to say: 'Well, it makes sense to me!' Interpretation is an attempt to 'fill in a figure'; it is the claim that I am able to fill in this or that figure. Interpretation usually becomes fulfilment if it is recognized and verified by the community. Fulfilment, therefore, can be seen as the art of *correct* understanding, correct interpretation and correct application. When Jesus fulfilled the figures, he annihilated, annulled the figures as figures. And if the figure is fulfilled, if it is indeed 'swallowed up', then it is lifted up to a higher eschatological reality.

The dialectics of figure and fulfilment, type and antitype, can also be illuminated with the analogy of question and answer. The figure is fulfilled, the type is completed by the antitype just as a question is annulled by an answer. But the fulfilled figure, the completed antitype or the answered question might create a new figure, a new type or a new question. And this new figure/type/question will have to be fulfilled also in due course. Accordingly, much of the tension of the Old Testament was removed when its figures were fulfilled, and most of its questions answered by the New Testament. It does not mean that there is no tension in Scripture any more: this new tension also waits for its fulfilment both by history and the individual.

Having looked at this dialectics of figure and fulfilment we are, perhaps, now in better position to understand what Auerbach said about 'figural interpretation':

> Figural interpretation establishes a connection between two events or persons, the first of which signifies not only itself but also the second, while the second encompasses or fulfils the first . . . Both, being real events or figures, are within time, within the stream of historical life. Only the understanding of the two persons or events is a spiritual act, but this spiritual act deals with concrete events whether past, present or future . . . since promise and fulfilment are real historical events, which either have happened . . . or will happen.[16]

Erich Auerbach and Leonard Goppelt are in perfect agreement when the former says that the understanding is a 'spiritual act' while the latter writes that typology is a *pneumatische Betrachtungsweise* ('spiritual understanding'). Goppelt further developed this view when he answered the attack of Bultmann, who seems to have misunderstood typology, conceiving it as a 'hermeneutical method' that has to do with the cyclical view of history to be observed in Oriental cultures or Greek philosophy. Against this distorted view Goppelt has maintained that: (1) typology was unknown in the non-biblical Hellenistic environment of early Christianity; (2) it was found exclusively in the Jewish environment but only as a principle of eschatology; (3) the typology that was found in Judaism had a prior history in the eschatology of the Old Testament.[17]

My purpose was to locate typology in the nature of biblical language. The fact that both Auerbach and Goppelt speak about understanding as a 'spiritual act' tends to confirm that typology is rooted in the metaphorical 'this is that' phase of the language.

Perhaps this is the reason why it seems to be so alien for people whose thinking is deeply rooted in scientific, logical and causal discourse. But only by this 'illogical' logic, by this reintepretation of the past, by this revisionary reading of the text can language be recreated.

To sum up, we can say that typology is a dynamic informing principle by which the imaginative elements of biblical language recreate themselves, and fulfilment language is a language that is able to recreate itself. Only the recreation of language can disclose a meaning that is invisible or hidden in the beginning but is going to be unfolded as time grows or progresses.

MEANING: FROM SEED TO PLANT

So far we have come to see that biblical language is fulfilment-language which means that this language is able to recreate itself ('my word . . . shall prosper in the thing whereto I sent it'). Such a fulfilment-language by its nature, gradually generates 'meaning' for the reader. I am proposing the thesis that meaning in the Bible tends to be a dynamic process rather than a static entity: meaning is *in statu nascendi*, it is gradually being born. But in order to understand this we must first discuss some traditional views of meaning in biblical language.

Now, what is the 'meaning' of the biblical words? In biblical studies exegesis is usually concerned with the exposition of meaning and the principles of exegesis are usually established by hermeneutics. Language and the interpretation of meaning are inseparable in the Bible as the Bible is not a scientific book describing historical events and presenting geographical, biological or other data. Fundamentalists, who claim that the Bible is inerrant even in respect to history, geography, or biology, share a descriptive-referential view of biblical language. They do not realize that the canonical biblical text is itself a strange mixture of events, earlier texts and even interpretation. The text itself is interpretation because it not only witnesses to certain events but also interprets them and even reinterprets earlier interpretation of texts and of events. Old Testament persons and events are reinterpreted in the light of the new eschatological event and they are seen differently in retrospect, in the light of Christ, the Messiah. Christ fulfils not only individual figures of the Old Testament but he fulfils the figure of 'Israel', as well as the figure of the 'Law' or the figure of 'Scripture', that is what we understand today as the Old Testament. By identifying himself with these figures he moves them on to a further stage of salvation history. 'Something greater is here' – says Jesus frequently in the Gospels. As we saw, this element is the *Steigerung*, which indicates that we have come to an advanced level of salvation history and everything that is behind us, should be seen from this perspective. This 'revisionary mode' is an inherent typological aspect of biblical language.

Once we appreciate this intricate complexity of biblical language, and that language is organically bound up with meaning, then we should not be surprised by twenty centuries of fierce debate between various interpretative communities about the 'sense' or 'senses' of biblical words.

It was felt quite early in the history of interpretation that a distinction can be made between the 'letter' and the 'spirit'; the first one determining the 'literal sense', and the second one the 'spiritual' sense. This demand for such a distinction claimed to go back to St Paul's dictum in 2 Corinthians 3:6:

> the letter killeth, but the spirit giveth life.

In the Middles Ages Thomas Aquinas also made a distinction between the literal sense and the spiritual sense. For him the literal sense is the one that the human author directly intended and which his *words* (*verba*) conveyed. The spiritual (sometimes called 'typical') sense is the meaning conveyed by the *things* (*res*). This thomistic-scholastic dualism has survived in Catholic exegesis up to the present day. In *The Jerome Biblical Commentary* (1968), for example, we can read:

The literal sense is:
The sense which the human author directly intended and which his words convey.
The spiritual (typical) sense is:
The deeper meaning that the things (persons, places and events) of Scripture possess because, according to the intention of the divine author, they foreshadow future things.[18]

This dualistic and rather rigid distinction of the senses has often led to an arbitrary allegorization, or, 'overspiritualization' of the words of the Bible. This tendency was especially strong when theologians tried to impose the categories of Greek philosophy on the Bible. This was the practice, for example, of the representatives of the School of Alexandria (Clement, Origen). These brilliant and highly educated minds wanted to explain the meaning of the biblical text in terms that were alien from it. Origen invented a threefold division of the senses according to the Pauline anthropology in 1 Thessalonians 5:23:

1. 'body': literal-historical sense
2. 'soul': moral-psychological sense
3. 'spirit': spiritual-allegorical-mystical sense[19]

Medieval hermeneutics is usually associated with the *Quadriga* or the 'four senses' of Scripture:

1. literal-historical
2. allegorical
3. moral
4. anagogical

This distinction, so popular in the Middle Ages, goes back probably to John Cassian (c. 365–c. 435). A little verse was invented about it probably as a mnemonic aid for students:

> Littera gesta docet, quid credas allegoria moralis quid agas, quo tendas, anagogia.[20]

> (The letter teaches the history, what you believe is allegory, what you act is morality, and where you are going is anagogy.)

Against this medieval idea of 'many senses' of Scripture the reformers claimed that there was only 'one sense', though it might be compound: literal and figurative.

Whilst in the Middle Ages the stress was on the spiritual-allegorical meaning of the biblical text, interest gradually shifted towards the literal-historical sense in the centuries following the Reformation. This tendency took a radical step forward in the eighteenth century with the birth of the historical-critical method. It is interesting to note that Roman Catholic theologians have only been able to adopt the literal-historical approach to the biblical text since it was sanctioned by the papal encyclical *Divino Afflante Spiritu* in 1943.

Over the centuries there have been many bitter conflicts between these two extreme tendencies: on the one hand 'spiritualistic' allegory-mindedness and on the other hand 'materialistic' literal-mindedness. Whilst medieval commentaries were packed with fanciful allegories, the twentieth-century reader of biblical scholarship is overwhelmed with thousands of volumes of historical criticism. Whilst in the Middles Ages the spiritual sense was favoured at the expense of the literal, today historical critics emphasise what they understand to be the 'literal' at the expense of the spiritual sense. (This shift towards the historical sense is most remarkable in the 1990 edition *The New Jerome Biblical Commentary*). But if we can find a new understanding of the literal sense, we can, in any case, transcend this artificial dichotomy or dualism between 'literal' and 'spiritual'. Dualistic concepts are alien from Scripture, they tend to be the products of a Platonic-Greek mentality. What is at issue here is how we can draw out meaning from within the very language of Scripture itself. If meaning is to correspond to the nature of fulfilment-language then this meaning should be seen also as a process and not as a static entity.

Brevard Childs in a recent article on the problem of *sensus literalis* has convincingly argued that the historical-critical method committed a fatal error when it tried to locate the literal meaning of the biblical text in its historical reference, therefore identifying the *sensus literalis* with the *sensus originalis*. The aim was apparently to reconstruct the original meaning by getting rid of the interpretative layers or myths. But, says Childs, in this way the integrity of the literal sense was in fact lost. When the literal sense is identical with the historical, meaning is to be found not 'within' but 'behind' the text. In this way, not only is the integrity of the literal sense denied, but the Bible loses its 'scope' or 'shape' as a concept of Scripture belonging to a community of faith. The historical-critical method resulted in some desperate attempts to bridge the huge gap between the historical meaning 'then' and the present significance 'now'. Childs demonstrates that the integrity of the literal sense can only be regained in the context of the 'canon', that is to say the Scripture of the community of faith. By regaining the integrity of the literal sense, the elements of 'shaping' (that took place under inspiration) can be reconstructed and only this can make the actualization possible again.

> The literal sense of the text is the plain sense witnessed to by the community of faith. It makes no claim of being the original sense or even of being the best. Rather, the literal sense of the canonical Scriptures offers a critical theological norm for the community of faith on how the tradition functions authoritatively for the future generations of the faithful.[21]

Childs' grand and heroic programme of 'relocating' the literal sense in the canon of Scripture finds a striking parallel in Northrop Frye's literary vision of the 'unity' and of the 'shape' of the Bible. Childs' effort to locate the literal sense of the text in the language of Scripture instead of in the external historical circumstances, is one of the attempts that aim to break down the artificial dichotomy between the extreme 'materialistic' (literalistic) and 'spiritualist' (allegorical) tendencies in interpreting Scripture. I shall invite four technical terms, each of them suggesting that in fulfilment-language meaning is not static (whether literal or spiritual) but it is in process, in constant motion, in oscillation between the poles of the literal and the spiritual. Whenever the historical sense is overemphasized (as nowadays) the spiritual aspect is to be stressed; whenever spiritualist-allegorical tendencies exclusively dominate (as in the Middle Ages) the historical sense must be defended. In the Bible, meaning, between these two poles, is in the making, in progress. The first term we shall have a look at is Frye's idea of polysemous meaning.

Polysemous Meaning

Frye condemns anti-intellectual 'populist' literalism in Christianity, which he associates with the demotic-descriptive phase of language but he nevertheless writes in *The Great Code*, that 'one of the central issues of the present book [is] the nature of "literal" meaning.'[22] How does he reconcile this apparent contradiction? He says that for the populist mind the literal meaning is identical with the descriptive meaning.[23] This view identifies meaning with the words' 'centrifugal' reference to the outside, 'real' world. Against this 'externalized literalism' Frye locates the literal meaning in the 'centripetal', *poetic* meaning which arises from the interconnection of words.[24] This literal meaning is warranted by the 'shape' of the Bible when read as a unity of narrative and imagery. However, this unity is realized only in reading. Only in reading do we experience meaning. To describe the effect of reading on meaning Frye has adopted Dante's term 'polysemous' meaning. This expression does not imply many different meanings nor does it contradict the primacy of the literal meaning. The reformers' and Milton's formula that 'No passage is to be interpreted in more than one sense' remains unchallenged. Frye describes what he means by this term as follows:

> One of the commonest experiences in reading is the sense of further discoveries to be made within the same structure of words. The feeling is approximately 'there is more to be got out of this', or we may say . . . that every time we read it we get something new out of it. This 'something new' is not necessarily something we have overlooked before, but may come rather from a new context in our experience . . .[25]

Commenting on Dante's four senses Frye writes:

> What is implied here is a single process growing in subtlety and comprehensiveness, not different senses, but different intensities or wider contexts of a continuous sense, unfolding like a plant out of a seed.[26]

With this idea of polysemous meaning Frye, like Childs, is able to preserve the integrity of the literal sense ('not different senses') and he is also able to avoid the trap of historicists or intentionalists who want to fix the meaning in an external, historical or biographical reality. There have been some other technical terms that, like Frye's 'polysemous meaning', have tried to provide room for this 'continuous sense'. What is common to all these theories is that meaning is not conceived as something static or fixed but rather as an ongoing, unfolding process, 'unfolding like a plant out of a seed'. If we conceive of the language of the Bible in terms of a 'seed', then meaning should also be understood as an organic growth.

Out of the following three parallel terms, two are taken from the history of medieval hermeneutics. The fourth term was invented by some Catholic theologians in our century. I am going to discuss briefly the term *theoria* as used by the representatives of the School of Antioch (fourth century); the term *sententia*, as used by Hugh of St Victor (twelfth century) and, in somewhat more detail, the *sensus plenior* (fuller sense), a term that gained currency in Catholic exegesis between 1950–1970.

Theoria ('Vision')

In the third century A. D. there was an elitist cathechetical school in Alexandria. Alexandria had been the centre of learning since the time of Philo (Christ's contemporary) and the intellectual climate of the place had always favoured an excessively allegorical interpretation of Scripture. Clement of Alexandria (c. 150–215) and Origen (c. 185–253) were convinced that every word and syllable of Scripture had a symbolical meaning to be deciphered. They also frequently applied typology but this typology was swallowed up by their Platonic allegorism. Clement, for example, adopted Philo's speculation about Isaac's name: the name means 'laughter' and thereby it is a mystical prophecy about Christ who would fill us with joy because of our own redemption. Origen was also firmly convinced that the prophecies are full of enigmatic and dark conceptions and therefore 'the mind of Christ' (1 Corinthians 2:16) is necessary to safeguard the people from lapsing into literalistic misreadings. Origen said that the Jews, the heretics (Marcion) and the primitive readers were taking the letter at its face-value without any regard to the 'spirit'. He ridiculed what he saw as the absurdities of a literal reading and of 'carnal' understanding in his comments on Genesis: it is impossible to imagine that God was literally walking in the Garden of Eden. But the New Testament abounds in similar examples. How absurd it is to imagine literally a mountain from which all the countries of the world could be seen (Matthew 4:8). Therefore 'Scripture has woven into the historical narrative some feature which did not happen . . .'[27] The problem with Origen is not his rejection of the absurdities of literalistic misreadings but his rejection of the historical reality of the prophecies and his ambition to approach meaning via Greek philosophy. This is the position that the School of Antioch reacted against a century later:

> People ask what the difference is between allegorical exegesis and historical exegesis. We reply that it is great and not small; just as the first leads to impiety, blasphemy and falsehood, so the

other is conformed to truth and faith. It was the impious Origen of Alexandria who invented this art of allegory.[28]

This quotation summarizes well the hostile attitude of the School of Antioch towards the allegorical practices of the Alexandrians. The representatives of this school were Diodore of Tarsus (d. 394), Theodore of Mopsuestia (c. 350–407) and John Chrysostom (c. 354–407). Diodore's best known works are his famous commentaries on the Psalms which contain significant hermeneutical remarks as well. He is also said to have written a treatise, now lost, on, *The Difference Between Theoria and Allegoria*. Fortunately his views can be reconstructed from his introduction to the Psalms.

In his commentary on the Psalms Diodore complains that people are not singing the Psalms intelligently and he warns his readers that they should sing the Psalms 'from the depth of their mind, not from shallow sentiments or just with the tip of their tongue'.[29] They are requested to pay attention to the meaning of the words, to the literal sense. Then he introduces his principle of *theoria* ('vision') which he formulated as a defence against allegory. This principle is firmly rooted in the historical reality of revelation.

> We will not shrink from the truth but will expound it according to the historical substance (*historia*) and the plain literal sense (*lexis*). At the same time, we will not disparage anagogy and their higher *theoria*. For history is not opposed to *theoria*. On the contrary, it proves to be the foundation and the basis of the higher senses ... *theoria* must never be understood as doing away with the underlying sense; it would then be no longer *theoria* but allegory.[30]

Diodore mentions that Paul used the term 'allegory' in Galatians 4:24 but he claims that Paul really meant *theoria*. Those who apply allegory are careless of the historical sense and merely follow their own imagination. But to repudiate allegorization should not mean the rejection of 'theorizing', that is, lifting the concept into a higher anagogy.

Theoria, says Diodore, is a middle-of-the-road approach: it frees us from both Hellenism, that reads alien elements into Scripture (later known as 'eisegesis') and also from the literalism of Judaism that keeps rigidly to the letter. He compares *theoria* to *tropologia* ('figuration') and to *parabole* (parabolic expression). This implies that the meaning does not lose its literal-historical reality by having a 'surplus', it carries also a potential future meaning. Thus a prophetic speech may correspond both to the time of the prophet and to the future as the divine words can be adapted in every moment, at any time. But he also warns the reader that 'the understanding of such a *theoria* must be left to those endowed with a fuller charism.'[31]

Sententia ('Deeper Sense')

This is a term used by Hugh of St Victor (d. 1142) the founder of the Victorine school in Paris. This school contributed much to the rediscovery of the literal sense of the Bible that had been suppressed for centuries by the dominant trends of allegorizations. Due to the industrious research of Beryl Smalley we have come to know much about the activity of this school and about its close connections with the followers of Rashi (d. 1105), the most significant Jewish exegete in Northern France.[32]

Hugh was a passionate opponent of baseless allegorizing and he repudiated those who despised the historical-literal meaning:

> I personally blame those who strive superstitiously to find a mystical sense and a deep allegory where none is, as much as those who obstinately deny it, when it is there.[33]

He emphasized throughout his works that good exegetes should always begin with the study of the literal or historical sense:

> Do not despise these lesser things. Those who despise the lesser things gradually fail. If you scorn to learn your alphabet, you will never even make your name as a grammarian.[34]

Hugh introduces the term *sententia* in his unique and unfortunately little known hermeneutical treatise: *Didascalicon On the Study of Reading*. For Hugh, understanding Scripture can be compared to the structure of a great building: its foundation is history and its superstructure is allegory.

> I am not now saying that you should first struggle to unfold the figures of the Old Testament and penetrate its mystical sayings before you come to the Gospel streams you must dream from.

But just as you see that every building lacking a foundation cannot stand firm, so also is it in learning. The foundation and principle of sacred learning, however, is history, from which, like honey from the honeycomb, the truth of allegory is extracted. As you are about to build, therefore, lay first the foundation of history; next, by pursuing the typical meaning; next, build up a structure in your mind to be a fortress of faith. Last of all, however, through the loveliness of morality, paint the structure over us with the most beautiful colours.[35]

Concerning the order of exposition Hugh observes three things: the letter (*littera*), the sense (*sensus*) and what is translated into English as 'deeper meaning' (*sententia*). The letter, he says, is sometimes perfect, sometimes compressed. So is the sense; it frequently seems to be unfitting or incongruous, especially if we isolate it from the context. It is frequently the case, he says, that 'things said according to the idiom of that language and which, although they are clear in that tongue, seem to mean nothing in our own.'[36] While the 'sense' may contain elements that disagree, the 'deeper meaning' (*sententia*),

> admits no contradiction, it is always harmonious, always true. Sometimes there is a single deeper meaning for a single expression; sometimes there are several deeper meanings for a single expression; sometimes there are several deeper meanings for several expressions.[37]

This deeper meaning also helps to create unity between the two testaments. With the help of this deeper meaning we are able to see that the Old Testament was fulfilled by Christ because he is both the Lion of Judah and the Slain Lamb who is alone worthy to open the seals of the book (Revelations 5:5–6). At the end of his treatise Hugh admonishes the reader with the notion of Augustine: it is not the thought of Scripture that is to be made identical with our (corrupt) way of thinking but 'we ought rather to wish our thought identical with that of Scripture'.[38]

The Sensus Plenior ('Fuller Sense')

We have proposed a dynamic 'meaning in process' concept to solve the tension between the literal-historical and the spiritual-allegorical senses. Our last auxiliary term to illustrate this concept is the *sensus plenior* ('fuller sense'). Moreover, all the four terms we are discussing here are flexible categories as they can mediate between the language of the text and the reader. Such 'continuous meanings' process the words 'into' the reader. These terms provide coherence for an intertextual and intratextual hermeneutics based on 'Language' – 'Meaning' – 'Reading'.

The *sensus plenior* (hereafter: SP) is a modern term. It was invented by Ferdinandez in 1925 but gained wider currency after the papal encyclical of 1943 encouraged Catholic theologians to adopt methods of critical and historical exegesis in the study of the Bible.[39] The category was intended to help in understanding of some messianic prophetic texts like Genesis 3:15; Isaiah 7:14; Hosea 11:1 and so on. The SP also 'represented an effort to define a separate sense of Scripture which would not conflict with historical criticism but which could encompass traditional interpretations and preserve their claim to the inherent authority of Scripture'.[40]

The most significant theological discussion of this question was presented by Raymond E. Brown, who proposed the following definition in 1955:

> the *sensus plenior* is that additional, deeper meaning, intended by God but not clearly intended by the human author, which is seen to exist in the words of the biblical texts (or a group of texts, or even a whole book) when they are studied in the light of further revelation or development in the understanding of revelation.[41]

Brown emphasized that the SP is not a new sense but it belongs to the literal sense; it is, as he later puts it, the *approfondissement* of the literal sense.[42] It is a necessary consequence of the traditional doctrine of inspiration and the so-called 'double-authorship' (human and divine) of Scripture. Thus Isaiah as the human author was not necessarily aware that he was uttering prophecy about the birth of Christ: the fuller or deeper meaning of the passage is uncovered in a later stage of revelation and Matthew has recorded this discovery. The fuller sense of Scripture is the literal sense that is pregnant with a future. The prophet does not simply 'foresee' the future. For him all the futurity is within the 'thing' but it is understood only later on the basis of the progressive revelation of God. SP is usually recognized in retrospect: just as in Jesus' lifetime the disciples were unable to understand some of their master's sayings (for example about the temple) or his actions (for example the footwashing) but

Jesus promised to send them the Paraclete who would enable them to understand these sayings and events. According to J. Coppens the 'evangelists themselves have developed the *sensus plenior* of the words of Christ; and the charism of inspiration guarantees the fidelity of this development to the original'.⁴³ Indeed most of the prophetic texts, from the protoevangelium (Genesis 3:15) onwards, can be seen as charged with a fuller sense. In 1955 Brown also hinted at the possibility that by virtue of the SP the church can justify, for example the development of liturgy or even some of the mariological dogmas. However, by 1968 Brown had accepted the criticism of this aspect of SP by a Protestant exegete, namely that *SP* should not be a 'tool of partisan apologetics and a peg to hang new doctrines on'.⁴⁴

It is interesting to note a change in Raymond Brown's position on this subject. Seeming to attribute less and less significance to this term over the years, his interest has moved towards the historical-literal sense. Indeed in a book on the recent history of Roman Catholic exegesis (1982) one can read: 'it is safe to say that the *sensus plenior* is a dead letter for nearly all Catholic exegetes.'⁴⁵

Thus the SP had only a short-lived career in Catholic exegesis. Among some Protestants, however, it soon gained currency. As early as in 1965 J. M. Robinson suggested that the SP should take the direction of the New Hermeneutics (Gadamer, Ebeling and so on) which rejects the idea of 'authorial intention' and conceives the text and its life from its original composition up till now as a 'word-event'.⁴⁶ It would imply that it is not the 'author' but the 'language' that speaks in texts. We shall come back to this point in connection with Ricoeur's view of the text in the following section on 'Reading'.

The term was creatively adopted by an American Protestant biblical scholar, William Sanford LaSor. He suggested the following definition:

> the fuller meaning of a passage, the 'something more' that was given by God in the divine inspiration, that makes the message equally valid as the word of God to succeeding generations.⁴⁷

LaSor related the SP to the 'prophecy and fulfilment pattern'. He rejected the idea that prophecy is a mere prediction of future events, claiming instead, that it is the 'revelation of God's purpose in the present situation and its on-going character. It is an age-long outworking of his own will.'[48] The idea of prophecy is that God is fulfilling his purpose which is not yet complete. Prophecy that

> reveals some part of God's redemptive purpose is capable of being filled, or achieving a fullness, so that when it is *filled full* it is *fulfilled*.[49]

The SP or the fullness of meaning can be discovered when we 'relate the situation and the prophecy to the ongoing redemptive purpose of God.'[50] LaSor also provided three short but very useful illustrations of how the SP can be discovered in three familiar passages: Genesis 3:15; Hosea 11:1; Micah 5:2. Let us quote the first one:

> And I will put enmity between thee and the woman, and between thy seed and her seed; it shall bruise thy head, and thou shall bruise his heel.

LaSor argued that the literal meaning does not make a great deal of sense and that a spiritualized reading would not say more than that we must seek to crush the source of our temptation. He explored the sense of the text as follows:

> The entire account (Genesis 3:14–19) contains two interwoven strands, one of which speaks of defeat, suffering, toil, and death, while the other speaks of future generations, of provision of food and sustenance of life, and the ultimate triumph over the serpent. The larger context tells of the satanic origin of temptation . . . and how yielding to it brought death upon the human race. The rest of the Bible tells how God is working to remove the results of this sin, and accomplish his redemptive purpose. The *sensus plenior* of the passage then can be discovered. I do not find the expression 'the seed of the woman' to be a prophecy of the Virgin Mary or the Virgin Birth, but I do find the fullness of meaning in some as-yet-unspecified member of the human race who would destroy the satanic serpent, thus playing a key role in God's redemptive plan. In that sense, the passage is indeed the first enunciation of the good news.[51]

LaSor's conclusion is that 'the quest for a *sensus plenior* is part of the discovery of the fullness of God's purpose in his revelation. It is the recognition that *at any moment he has the end in view and in any generation he has the future generations in His purpose.*'[52]

A reader encountering Matthew's Gospel for the first time might be somewhat perplexed by the author's claim that, for example, Isaiah 7:14 or Hosea 11:1 were being fulfilled by Christ. But armed with our new understanding of the nature of biblical language as 'fulfilment-language' and with the recognition of how the SP is at work in the text our first perplexity may well dissolve. Matthew's Gospel recreates the Old Testament passage, it 'fills in' the 'hollow mould' of the enigmatic text. The meaning has been there for centuries but it comes to fullness, according to Matthew, only in Christ. For him this Old Testament passage is like a 'seed'. A 'seed' contains the tree and the branches in potential yet no scientific-microscopic analysis could demonstrate all that the seed carried. The 'surplus' of meaning, the 'fullness' of a passage, the SP can only be recognized in due course, when the time is 'ripe' for the new revelatory activity of God. This activity is a process, proceeding towards a fullness and when it is completed, it is 'full', 'filled' in other words 'fulfilled'.

The SP can be applied creatively within the 'canonical approach'. With the help of the SP as a hermeneutical method one can discern 'in a text all the strata of meaning that the canonical context warrants. The progress of revelation dictates that the meaning of scriptural texts became deeper and clearer as the canon unfolded'.[53] However, critics of the SP are probably right when they say that this theory of the SP is based on a traditional view of inspiration which attributed intention to the author alone. However, I believe that the SP remains a useful category even for a new, reader-oriented theory of inspiration. In order to develop this new idea further we must turn to the question of reading.

READING: EATING THE BOOK

At the beginning I suggested that typology is a way of reading the Bible. But what is 'reading'? How is it related to 'language' and 'meaning', how is this threefold hermeneutical scheme accomplished in reading?

Concerning biblical language we have come to the conclusion that it is not a scientific-descriptive language because it implies interpretation. The biblical text could, perhaps, be reduced to the formula: event + interpretation. But what, then, is interpretation? Perhaps we may say that man is *homo interpretans*, a being, who continuously perceives, understands and interprets the world around him. Interpretation is a stance, a perspective, a conviction, indeed, a synonym for belief. As we have seen, events are not only interpreted but reinterpreted in the Bible. Therefore typology, this 'revisionary mode', is an inherent aspect of biblical language. Now if biblical language is interpretative language and if interpretation is a synonym for belief, then this language can also be called the language of belief. From whence is this belief? It is here that we confront the problem of Scriptural inspiration.

Dogmatic and traditional hermeneutics usually explained the question of inspiration as follows: on the basis of 2 Timothy 3:16 and 2 Peter 1: 20-21 we can speak about a 'double authorship' of Scripture. The ultimate author of Scripture is God who 'breathed out' (*theopneustos*) his word and the historical authors were the prophets, the holy men of God who wrote under the influence of the spirit. Some fundamentalists might add that these texts are inerrant as they were written under the Spirit of God. For this traditional, 'precritical' hermeneutics, the text is the individual author's property whether this individual is God ('the book of the Lord': Isaiah 34:16) or the individual prophet, and the text's meaning is determined by the authorial intention.

Critical or historical hermeneutics is based on the assumption that most books of the Bible cannot be attributed, as they used to be, to individual authors, because the texts are the results of a long process of (re-)creation. The final work can be attributed to the continuous efforts of generations of authors and redactors. The text in this hermeneutics is also the author's 'property', but the 'author' is an invisible community of redactors through the centuries. If there is room for inspiration in this context at all, then the community is to be seen as an 'inspired' entity.

It has been our concern to reflect upon the limits of the historical-critical method. Therefore we may now ask: is there a 'postcritical' theory of inspiration? If our postcritical, hermeneutic method is rooted in language then we have to find the working of inspiration also in language. I have gained some assistance in the development of my ideas from a brilliant article on this subject by Walter Vogels.

Vogels offers indeed a postcritical theory of inspiration which he calls 'Inspiration in a Linguistic Mode'.[54] His main thesis is that due to modern research in linguistics, semiotics and hermeneutics on the nature and identity of the text we have to rethink our views of inspiration. While in oral communication there are only two realities: the speaker and the listener, in written communication there are three realities: the writer, the text and the reader. The text is the object of two activities: writing and reading. However, once the text is written, the writer has no authority over the text, and the text becomes a reality in itself, the property of the reader. The text permits several readings but resists other readings. Reading is a *rewriting* of the text – it is a creative activity as rewriting is recreation. 'A text is an open reality always stimulating new readings.'[55] Reading is, therefore giving new life to a text, while respecting it.

Inspiration in this view is a *quality of the text* and it is not the result of authorial intention, whether the author is an individual (pre-criticism) or a community (criticism). The inspiration of the text is recognized only in reading.[56] The text has the quality of inspiration because it was written with the assistance of the Spirit.

> The Bible is not inspired because people decide so, on the contrary, it is just the opposite. The text itself, thanks to its special production, has a quality which makes the text capable of stimulating and nourishing the faith of readers throughout the centuries . . . The reading community always gives the Bible new meanings because the Bible as text is always open to new insights.[57]

Vogels stresses that the text of the Bible 'grows' with the growth of the believing community. His most genuine insight is the recognition that the human-divine text (just as any other text) can be read because the text respects certain structures that are common to the writer and the reader. If so, then the Spirit that was at work in writing must equally be at work in reading. The consequence of this insight is that if we say, 'God is the author of the Bible' we must immediately add that 'God is the reader of the Bible'. 'Just as the God-author did write through human writers, so does the God-reader read through human readers.'[58] Vogels convincingly shows the passage in 2 Timothy 3:16 – namely, that 'All Scripture is inspired by God . . . ' – can be translated as 'All Scripture inspired by God and inspiring, i.e. infusing God . . . '[59]

Reading as Appropriation

Vogels' linguistic view of inspiration is rooted, as we have seen, in a postcritical theory of the text. What then exactly is this postcritical theory of the text? Paul Ricoeur, whose name is virtually emblematic of what is usually meant by the term 'postcriticism' puts forward an important theory of the text in his article 'What is a Text?'[60] Ricoeur maintains that the text replaces the dialogue where the act of writing is parallel to the act of reading. In the text the dialogue is intercepted but it does not mean that the text is without reference. In the text the reference is only deferred, and in this sense we can speak about the 'suspension' of the text. Ricoeur distinguishes two kinds of readings: 'explanation' and 'interpretation'. In the first case, he says, we remain in the suspense of the text, and consider it worldless, authorless, and explain its structure. In the second case we have got to do with interpretation which means that we remove the text's suspense and accomplish it. The ideal reading is the one which maintains the tension between explanation and interpretation, and these two approaches should, therefore, not be seen as conflicting with one another (Dilthey) but rather as complementing one-another.

Ricoeur's next step is to work out a new theory of interpretation. To do this, he introduces one of his key-terms: 'appropriation'. We speak about appropriation, he says, when 'the interpretation of the text ends up in the interpretation of the subject',[61] when the text is 'completed' (we can even say: 'fulfilled' or, even 'satisfied'!) if the reader better understands himself. Interpretation overcomes estrangement or the cultural distance in so far as it appropriates ('swallows up') what was alien before.

In his *Interpretation Theory* he defines it as follows:

> Appropriation . . . ceases to appear as a kind of possession, as a way of taking hold of things, instead it implies a moment of dispossession of the egoistic and narcissistic ego.[62]

Moreover, interpretation as appropriation is also a kind of actualization and thus reading can be compared to the performance of a musical score. In the actualization of the text, reading becomes like speech. Interpretation should appropriate not the intention of the author but the intention of the text. The essence of Ricoeur's new theory of interpretation is that the text itself has intention: the text speaks, the text orientates our thought. Therefore interpretation is not an act on the text but of the text. Appropriation is the recovery of what is at work, in labour, in the text. Reading is only resaying what the text says by itself, it is an act in which the destiny of the text is 'fulfilled'.

Now we have come to see what a huge difference there is between 'usurpation' and 'appropriation'. Was Harold Bloom right in saying that the writers of the 'New' Testament not only 'misread' the so-called 'Old' Testament but they audaciously 'usurped' the strong poetry of the Hebrew Bible? How can we suggest that Bloom is mistaken? We can try to support our argument by making clearer the semantic difference between the two words. What is the meaning of 'usurpation'? The word undoubtedly evokes the feverish ambition of possession and this ambition has definitely to do with the hardening of one's ego ! 'Appropriation', as we have understood it from Ricoeur, is exactly the reverse: 'a moment of dispossession of the egoistic and narcissistic ego.' Appropriation is like 'swallowing up' or digesting something that was originally alien from us. Perhaps that is the reason why the Angel says to the Seer of Patmos in the Book of Revelation:

> Take it, and eat it up; it shall make thy belly bitter, but it shall be in thy mouth sweet as honey. (10:9)

My conclusion is, that a fulfilment of the biblical text in reading, ideally results in the loss of the ego. Now this is the very point where Ricoeur's theory of the text and Frye's vision of the Bible coincide. Frye writes:

> At the end [of the Bible] the reader, also, is invited to identify himself with the book . . . The apocalypse is the way the world looks after the ego has disappeared.[63]

This identification is probably due to the kerygmatic language and the authority of Scripture. The Bible has indeed a special authority. We remember Auerbach's almost military image of the Bible-stories that seek to subject us, and if we refuse to be subjected we are rebels.[64]

This declarative sentence is both true and false at the same time. It is true because it understands the authoritative claim of Scripture but it is false because it depicts this claim as an alien, totalitarian threat to man. It is exactly this Ricoeurian notion of appropriation that Auerbach, unlike Frye, failed to take into consideration. Frye, quoting Milton, can therefore assert that by the end of the Bible the ultimate authority is not the 'external Bible', but the Word of God in the human heart.[65] Only when the book is indeed 'swallowed up' can we speak about the disappearance of the ego. Paraphrasing Frye's notion about the purpose of studying Shakespeare, we can say that the end of reading the Bible is not to admire it but to possess it so that its verbal energy can filter into us and shape our way of thinking. Such an 'interpenetration' is the true purpose of reading the Bible.

However, Frye does not only speak about a 'moment' of dispossession like Ricoeur, but about an eventual final vision that is conveyed to us by the language of love, in which there is no ego, no argument, nor 'Old', nor 'New' Testament, in which life is not opaque but becomes transparent. It is the appropriation of the surprising final vision of the Seer of Patmos: namely, that the strong, victorious Lion of the tribe of Judah and the weak Lamb pitifully slain, are one.

3

Reading Scripture

THE UNITY OF SCRIPTURE

In Chapter 2 we have seen that typology as a linguistic phenomenon has to be completed in reading. Our conclusion was that every reading is both a rewriting and an interpretation of the text. We have also seen that the text itself was interpretation and that interpretation was an act 'of' the text rather than an act 'on' the text. The text is in action if it is inspired, and inspiration is not the result of authorial intention but a quality of the text. If the text is inspired by God, it also inspires God, it inspires a reading in tune with its writing: if the ultimate 'author' was God, then the ultimate 'reader' of the text is God as well.

In this Chapter the reader is invited to join my reading of Scripture. By 'Scripture' I mean the 'Christian Bible' as it has been a major informing and inspiring book of Western culture. As a student of English literature I have chosen to refer to the translation of the Bible which has had greatest influence on English writers and poets to date. This version is the King James Bible (1611), or Authorized Version.

However, the following reading is based on some assumptions. First of all, this is going to be a layman's reading and not a professional theologian's. I am reading Scripture by following the canonical rather than the chronological-historical order of books. I consciously adopt this naive or unscholarly attitude for two reasons. First, I wish to demonstrate that the Bible definitely has a beginning and an end and, despite the obstacles, a linear-sequential reading is possible. Secondly, poets and writers read Scripture also in an unscholarly manner and they have made sense of it. The purpose of my reading is to help my readers envisage typological patterns emerging from the texts. Being a literary critic rather than a biblical scholar I shall draw on the works of such excellent theologians as Gerhard von Rad and Oscar Cullmann and I shall rely heavily on the classic work of Leonard Goppelt.

If the claim to read Scripture instead of concentrating on one or two certain books *of* Scripture seems too ambitious, my reason is that I wish to keep the totality or unity of Scripture in mind as the Bible is a typologically constructed book itself. It is worth considering Northrop Frye's notion of the 'sevenfold phases of revelation': Creation – Exodus – Law – Wisdom – Prophecy – Gospel – Apocalypse. His suggestion is that each 'phase' is the type of the one following it and the antitype of the one preceeding it. But while keeping this totality in mind, I shall have to be selective to some extent while trying to explore some rhetorical patterns or the frequently occuring figures that constitute the typological structure of Scripture. Before we begin our reading, some words must be said about the unity of Scripture.

Typology and Salvation History: Principles of Unity

The Bible is undoubtedly a collection of diverse books written within a span of more than 1000 years in various genres and styles, by authors of different social rank, education, temper, and piety. Nevertheless these writings have been moulded into 'one book' through the centuries. Nowadays the dominant historical and analytical approach emphasizes the diversity, complexity and idiosyncrasy of each book. However, if one is endowed with some artistic sensitivity then it is impossible not to notice a striking unity within the diversity. It is somewhat ironic that today, in the age of an extremely departmentalized academic biblical scholarship, it is the task of the literary critic to call attention to the intrinsic and imaginative unity of the Bible, an idea that has been neglected by the majority of biblical scholars.

Wherein, then, lies the 'unity of the Bible'? According to Frye the unity of the Bible consists 'in its ordering of words under the rubrics of typological, metaphorical and stylistic unity which comprehends an encyclopaedic and imaginative vision of the world from creation to apocalypse'.[1] For Frye then, the Bible is a great 'archetypal structure' and an 'encyclopaedic form'; the most obvious indication of its unity is its typological formation and construction. However, there is perhaps another agent, of equal significance, which plays a major role in the intrinsic and the imaginative unity of the Bible. This is the notion of *Heilsgeschichte* (salvation history) which implies a progressive understanding of revelation. The term was first used by some German theologians in the last century and revived in a different theological context by the Swiss Protestant theologian, Oscar Cullmann. He notes that typology and salvation history are two principles that are interrelated and interdependent, each of them conditioning the other.

> every presentation of the history of salvation . . . offers just one excerpt of the whole and draws out just certain lines of salvation history. Thus far, hardly any distinction exists between salvation-historical exposition and typology. Conversely, typology presupposes a wider salvation-historical framework and connects two points of this background. In typology, however, the connection is limited to two points being dealt with. Those parts and members of the salvation history which fall in between the points are either passed over or are not considered in this manner of confrontation.[2]

Cullmann also contended that though salvation history and typology are linked with the pattern of 'promise and fulfilment', typology nevertheless 'lacks the element of development'.[3] But we may challenge this view by appealing to Goppelt's idea of *Steigerung* ('heightening') which does imply the notion of 'development': a simultaneous leap forward and upward. *Steigerung* is 'like a shift of music into a new key as it crescendoes to a climax'.[4]

TYPOLOGY IN THE OLD TESTAMENT

Typology gained recognition in Old Testament studies when Gerhard von Rad published his programmatic essay in 1952: 'Typological Interpretation in the Old Testament'[5] which led to the revival of typology in biblical studies. He gave an even fuller treatment of this subject in his *Theology of the Old Testament*.[6] In von Rad's view typology is not a theological device but 'typological thinking is an elementary function of all human thought and interpretation'[7] and without this analogical way of thinking there would be no poetry. But typology in the Old Testament is totally different from the analogical thinking of the ancient Orient because in the Bible it is determined by the eschatological significance of the correspondance between the beginning and the end (*Urzeit – Endzeit*) and therefore von Rad doubts Bultmann's view that typology is based on the repetition deriving from a cyclic view of time. He prefers to use the term 'correspondence' (either temporal or spatial) instead of 'repetition'. As he says, the Old Testament is not a static book of facts but it is a book of prophetic faith with a radical openness and expectation towards the future. It is a book in which history becomes prophetic and all events are viewed in relation to the redemptive act of God: 'history becomes word and word becomes history'.[8] For von Rad typological interpretation should be concerned with the *kerygma* and it should interpret events as being in preparation: the whole Old Testament is a witness to Christ.[9] Contrary to the former practice of typology which saw the types (persons, events, institutions) as being static and objective, von Rad revived a typology which has a 'keener eye for history' and has more affinity with the modern theological tradition. He worked with the idea of a dynamic typology of events: typological correspondences can be discerned only by faith; it is an interpretation based on faith's witness to past events. If God's dealings with his people are witnessed to, 'the possibility exists of seeing in this a shadow of the New Testament revelation of Christ'.[10] Von Rad does not assert naively that certain Old Testament characters or events 'foreshadowed' something of the future but maintains that in retrospect, in the light of faith, these things can indeed be seen to have foreshadowed something of the future. While for some nineteenth century theologians such as Fairbairn, typology was a part of the divine revelation which is analogous to an educational process 'leading mankind progressively to the fullness of time',[11] in von Rad's view, typology is not a part of the divine revelation any more but is a kind of theology, or, at least, a common mode of human thought employed by the theologians of Israel and by the early Christians. Thus for him typology does not belong to the *historia revelationis* but to the *historia theologiae*. For him it was a useful theological method by which he understood and proclaimed God's self-revelation in history.[12]

Typology has also been revived by Jewish scholars. In his thorough book on *Biblical Interpretation in Ancient Israel*[13] Michael Fishbane justified the 'inner-biblical typologies', the 'homological' likeness of events or persons in the Hebrew Bible. He envisaged four kinds of typologies within the Hebrew Bible: (1) Typologies of Cosmological – Historical Nature: ('New heaven and New earth'); (2) Typologies of Historical Nature: (Exodus – Conquest) (3) Typologies of Spatial Nature: (Eden, Temple); (4) Typologies of Biographical Nature (Adam, Noah, Moses, Joshua and so on).[14] He pointed out that some fixed rhetorical terms, like *'Just* as . . . *so'* are used to establish a typological relationship between two persons, for example:

> The Lord said unto Joshua . . . 'as I was with Moses, so I will be with thee.' (Joshua 3:7)

Though typology becomes manifest especially in the prophetic books of the Old Testament, we can also detect the origins of this mode of thought in the historical narratives of the Pentateuch. Typology in Genesis is, of course, far from the sophisticated typology in Pauline theology but the idea of the 'new' being interpreted in terms of the 'old', the sense of an advance by repetition is definitely present on the first pages of the Bible. For the Jewish mind the future is inseparable from the past as progress can take place only in terms of remembering.

Recurring Patterns of Blessing in Genesis

If one reads the Bible straight from the very beginning, one soon becomes aware of certain repeated patterns. One example of such a pattern is the blessing of God, given to those with whom he initiates a partnership.

Adam – Noah

Verbal features establish a direct typological link between Adam and Noah. Thus Noah is a 'new Adam' who is asked to preside over a restored world after the flood. God blessed Adam after his creation with the following words:

> Be fruitful, and multiply, and replenish the earth, and subdue it: and have dominion over the fish of the sea, and over the fowl of the air, and over every living thing that moveth upon the earth. (1:28)

After the flood, when God 'recreates' the world, he gives the blessing to Noah with the same pattern of words:

> 'Be fruitful and multiply, and replenish the earth. And the fear of you and the dread of you shall be upon every beast of the earth,

and upon every fowl of the air, upon all that moveth upon the earth, and upon all the fishes of the sea; into your hand they are delivered.' (Genesis 9:1-2)

Adam – Abraham

The New Testament is particularly concerned with the typological significance of Abraham as the 'father' of all believers (Romans 4:11), who was also called the 'Friend of God' (James 2:23). But in Genesis itself he appears to be much more than a 'hero' of a historical narrative. Through Noah, God was able to renew his covenant with man following the flood. After another cataclysm, that is, the fall of Babel, Abram is chosen to be God's human partner in his unfolding plan of redemption. So the partnership, or covenant, is restored and renewed again. The pattern of blessing is again repeated, God promises Abram the gifts of land, seed and earthly blessing (12:1-3):

> 'Get thee out of thy country . . . unto a land that I will shew thee: And I will make thee a great nation, and make thy name great and thou shalt be a blessing . . . in thee shall all families of the earth be blessed.'

Fishbane noted: 'In this typological context, it cannot fail to strike one that these three blessings are, in fact, a typological reversal of the primordial curses in Eden: directed against the earth, human generativity, and human labour.'[15]

'Type-Scenes' in Genesis

Besides the typological parallels between individuals, there is also an interesting repetition of some patterns and themes already within the patriarchal narratives. Robert Alter calls such recurring patterns 'biblical type-scenes' borrowing the term from Homer-scholarship. The notion is that

> there are fixed situations which the poet is expected to include in his narrative and which he must perform according to a set order of motifs – situations like the arrival, the message, the voyage, the assembly, the oracle, the arming of the hero, and some half-dozen others.[16]

Such descriptive devices cannot always be found in the Bible therefore reference of this term in the Bible is somewhat different. We are going to discuss two 'type-scenes'. These are recurring narrative patterns within *Genesis*, but the first pattern especially has a significance extending far beyond *Genesis* itself.

The Recurring Pattern of 'Primogeniture'

One of the most significant recurring patterns in the Bible is the pattern of 'Primogeniture', the question of the first-born. The pattern begins in Genesis but runs through the whole Bible. *Primogeniture* originally involved the passing of the rights of inheritance to the firstborn son. In the Bible this pattern works in a special way. There is a peculiar emphasis on the passing over of the rights and the status of the firstborn son in favour of a younger one. Adam's firstborn son, Cain becomes a murderer. Abraham's eldest son Ishmael is passed over in favour of Isaac; Isaac's eldest son Esau is passed over in favour of Jacob; Jacob's eldest son, Reuben is passed over in favour of Judah; Joseph's eldest son Manasseh is passed over in favour of Ephraim. But the pattern is at work far beyond the book of Genesis. Moses and the entire first generation of Israel are denied entry to the Promised Land and the leadership is transfered to Joshua. The pattern proceeds into the history of Israel: though Saul was chosen by God to be the first king, God nevertheless passes over Saul and his heirs in favour of David.

St Paul perceived the expansion of this pattern in the history of the chosen people and in Galatians 4 he claimed that the Jews had been passed over in the same way in favour of the Christians. Hagar and Ishmael stand for the law, bondage, Mount Sinai and the 'flesh'. Thus 'allegorically' (or typically) they represent Judaism while Sarah and Isaac are figuring the gospel, freedom, Jerusalem, the promise, and thus they represent Christianity.

What is the significance of the typological symbolism of primogeniture in the Bible? Northrop Frye, who devoted an illuminating lecture to this subject said[17] that the Bible's emphasis on the passing over of the status of the firstborn in favour of a younger son represents a direct intervention of the divine breaking in upon the human sense of continuity. Jesus fills in the role of the firstborn and represents also the continuity of the line of David. The divine breaking in 'subverts' the continuity, and Jesus is shown not to be the natural son of Joseph, the descendant of David. Nevertheless he fulfilled this continuity through the direct divine intervention of the Virgin Birth. This involves the whole paradoxical conception of Christ, because Christ, as Frye says, 'is born after flesh like Ishmael but also after the promise of Isaac. So that his birth in the line of David . . . fulfils the law of primogeniture, but his actual birth represents a divine entry into history'.[18]

A Recurring Episode

There is an interesting, if bizarre, pattern that crops up three times in Genesis. This pattern is a unique manifestation of intertextuality within Genesis. In Genesis 12:10–20 we read that Abram travelled to Egypt to avoid famine and that while he was there he asked his wife Sarai to pretend that she was his sister and not his wife. He did this as he was afraid that he would be killed because of the beauty of his wife. When the men of Pharaoh catch sight of Sarai, she is taken to Pharaoh's house. Abram, in return, is treated well. Then, we are told, the Lord sent plague to Pharaoh and his house because of Sarai. When Pharaoh learns of Sarai's true identity, he asks Abram: 'Why didst thou not tell me that she was thy wife?' Then Abraham is sent away with Sarai and with all their goods.

The same situation recurs in another setting: in Genesis 20 we read that Abraham and Sarah travelled to Gerar and once again Abraham says that Sarah is his sister. The King of Gerar, Abimelech, takes Sarah to his house but Sarah's identity is revealed to him in a dream. Abimelech who had not touched Sarah, returns her to Abraham the following morning. But whilst in the previous incident Pharaoh's question was apparently a rhetorical one to which Abram did not reply, here Abimelech's question seems genuinely concerned with the motivation of Abraham's deed and Abraham defends his integrity: he says he had thought he would be killed because of his wife and he argues that Sarah was indeed his sister on his father's side. Due presumably to this sincere confession, there is a mutual reconciliation: Abraham is entertained in the land of Abimelech. He even prays to God for Abimelech's wife and maidservants and as a result of his prayer, their barrennes, imposed on them because of Sarah, is taken away.

The situation recurs for the third time in Genesis 26: 1–11. This time it is Isaac and his wife Rebekah who also settle down in Gerar. Similarly, out of fear, Isaac pretends that the fair-faced Rebekah is his sister and not his wife. In this version there is no hint that she is taken away to entertain the host of the place, but it is said that Abimelech, the king of the Philistines looked out of a window and saw Isaac and Rebekah involved in an embrace that was clearly more than fraternal! Abimelech therefore calls Isaac and asks him 'how saidst thou, She is my sister?' Isaac admits that he was afraid that he would die because of her. Abimelech is horrified because, as he says, 'one of the people might lightly have lien with thy wife' – which, he believes, would have brought guiltiness to the people. Then Abimelech commands that nobody should touch either Isaac or his wife.

So we have here what is substantially the same episode recurring three times in somewhat different settings. It makes sense to see these, not as historical episodes recorded in Genesis but as three versions of a 'proto'-story and for the literary critic the repetion of patterns or episodes is significant. We perceive an accelerating rhythm in the narration: the recurring 'old' pattern or formula tends to generate 'new' insights and meanings. The logic of typology is at work here: we understand the new in terms of the old.

Typology beyond the Pentateuch: Moses – Joshua

Typology points not only beyond Genesis but even beyond the Pentateuch. We might even ask whether the whole concept of 'Deuteronomy' as 'second law' or the 'repetition of the law' could also be conceived as a typological notion. And further on, could we perhaps conceive the relationship between the Pentateuch and the Book of Joshua as again a typological relationship and thereby justify the claim for the 'Hexateuch'? There is one level where typology is undoubtedly at work within the Hexateuch: this is the personal level. Therefore we now turn to the Moses-Joshua typology. Michael Fishbane has shown that salvific moments of Israelite history put on prototypical patterns which were then reiterated in the presentation of other or later events – the new was shown in terms of the old. So an historical event or a person could serve as 'the prototype for the descriptive shaping of the other'.[19] This is quite evident in the typological parallels between the Exodus and the Conquest or between Moses and Joshua.

Joshua is not just a new leader of the people but also a 'new Moses'. 'The Just . . . as . . . so' rhetorical formula is frequently applied to Joshua: 'as I was with Moses, so I will be with thee' (3:7);

'all Israel . . . feared him, as they feared Moses' (4:14). Before the destruction of Jericho, Joshua came face to face with a man holding his sword drawn against him. When Joshua inquired whether he was a friend or an enemy, and the man replied that he was 'a captain of the host of the Lord' and commanded Joshua in exactly the same words as the 'I am what I am' commanded Moses in the burning bush:

> Loose thy shoe from off thy foot; for the place whereon thou standest is holy. (5:15)

The crossing of the Jordan is also a typological reiteration of the crossing of the Red Sea. The 'just as . . . so' formula is applied also for the parallel between the Exodus and the Conquest: 'For the Lord your God dried up the waters of Jordan from before you, until ye were passed over, as the Lord your God did to the Red sea, which he dried up from before us, until we were gone over' (4:23).

Thus the crossing of the Jordan is virtually a replay of the crossing of the Red Sea. For the writer this event again testifies to the greatness of God. The people of Israel were interested in the depth of the meaning of the event and not in the descriptive logic of 'wie es eigentlich gewesen ist' (as it really happened). This is illustrated by the fact that these two crossings (and the two 'waters': the Red Sea and the Jordan) are being *fused* in the mind of the Psalmist when he praises the mighty things of God.

> When Israel went out of Egypt, the house of Jacob from a people of strange language; Judah was his sanctuary, and Israel his dominion. The sea saw it, and fled: Jordan (!) was driven back. (Psalm 114:1–3)

Typology in the Prophetic Texts

So far our concern has been to show that typology was already at work in the historical narratives at the beginning of the Bible. We have dwelt on this at some length as scholars have tended to overlook typology within the Pentateuch and the historical books. Von Rad and his followers emphasize that typology becomes manifest within the prophetic books. When the prophets announced that a new saving act was taking place in history they used the language of the old traditions in which they found some predictive character: 'new David', 'new Exodus' and the like. They saw the new in terms of the old and interpreted the old in the light of the new. The 'recitals of the old confessions' meant the 'reactualizing' of old events. To give some examples: Isaiah uses the Garden of Eden as a new paradise (9:1–2; 11:6–9); Hosea predicts another period in the wilderness (2:14–15; 12:9–10). Second Isaiah expects a new Exodus (43:16–21; 48:20–21; 51:9–11). David is often seen as typical of the King who is to come in the future (Isaiah 11:1; 51:3–4; Jeremiah 23:5; Ezekiel 34:23–24; Amos 9:11).

A literary critic, A. C. Charity, has convincingly demonstrated that the core of the Old Testament typology is the dialectic tension between the 'new' and the 'steadfast': God does not change but nevertheless he always creates something new. He encounters his people only in history, in the 'saving events'. Therefore Israel's confessions are always purely historical. God reveals himself primarily in history and not in nature (as in the pagan cults), nor in metaphysics (as in Greek philosophy). Playing with words we can, perhaps, say that while the pagan religions 'naturalized history', Israel, on the contrary, 'historicized' even nature. This radical historicity is the basis of the Old Testament typology. For Israel the continuous reciting of the past was both a contemporization and an actualization. The function of typology, as Charity asserts, has always been to confront man with God, to summon him for new decisions because the past provides analogical patterns for the future. For Charity typology is not a 'system' but a category of 'existentialist' concern, as in it the past is 'applied' to the needs of the present. God's mighty acts in the past are meant to summon God's people in the present for a new 'decision' and therefore typology is more 'imperative' than 'indicative':

> Only by living up to the imperative could each man affirm the indicative as applying to him, and to become what, by virtue of the act of God, he already was: a member of God's chosen people, living in the new history which God had given him, according to the way which God had shown him.[20]

It is interesting to note that typology is more evident in the 'weal'-prophecies than in the 'woe'-prophecies. Typology in the Old Testament already works within the framework of the 'promise and fulfilment' structure. Historical events are presented by the prophets 'in such relation to one another that they may be perceived to be purposive acts of God, tending towards fulfilment'.[21]

Some of the prophecies were already fulfilled within the Old Testament but due to Israel's disobedience, God's plan will not be accomplished with them. As this becomes more and more of a threatening possibility, the prophets are beginning to talk about a 'righteous remnant'. From the time of the Elijah stories (1 Kings 19:18) there is a growing belief that a small eschatological community will be the foundation-stone of God's new building (Isaiah 28:16). The remnant live in a provisional form of existence, their function is to point 'towards something still to come and still veiled'.[22] They prefer a future, eschatological reality, when the covenant with God, hitherto only half – lived, will be lived wholly and will be accomplished. A representative of this remnant is the 'righteous sufferer' or the 'suffering servant' of Deutero-Isaiah. The focus, we can see, is gradually narrowing down, first to the remnant and then to a single person. There is a sense of growing expectation and the Old Testament remains radically open. There is no attempt yet to remove the tension this created. The destiny of Israel will be, as Irenaeus used to say, 'recapitulated' by one person eagerly awaited but unrecognized and in the event, rejected. The message of old, its completion long awaited, will, similarly unnoticed, be fulfilled.

It has been suggested that typology in the Old Testament reaches its culmination in Deutero-Isaiah. Here we can observe both a cosmological and a historical typology. For the first – cosmological typology – we can say that the author promises a creation anew: 'For, behold, I create new heavens and new earth' (65:17). Then the present state of the world, which is 'wilderness' will become like Eden (51:3). Deutero-Isaiah envisages a divine healing that will take place in the heart of creation. Therefore there is a strong parallel between 'primordial time' (*Urzeit*) and eschatological time (*Endzeit*). Fishbane observes that the central historical events of Israel are also perceived as 'the reiteration of foundational cosmic patterns from a prehistorical period',[23] and his interesting conclusion is that the 'reiteration of cosmic prototypes in historical time results in the historicization of myth'.[24] Deutero-Isaiah frequently used the terms 'first things', 'new things' or 'things to come'. For him the *Endzeit* is like the *Urzeit* as he is 'the first and the last' (44:6), and that is the reason why he can declare the end from the beginning (46:10):

I have declared the former things from the beginning; and they went forth out of my mouth, and I shewed them I did them suddenly, and they came to pass. (48:3)

This eschatological-cosmological typology illustrates the way in which the 'word' is at work in fulfilment-language: the word is 'loosed off' and it is in motion until it reaches its goal and destination. When it reaches whom it was sent to, the word is fulfilled.

Turning now to the historical-eschatological typology in Deutero-Isaiah, we can see how much of this is related to the Exodus-experience. B. W. Anderson shows that there are numerous linguistic echoes of the Exodus tradition in Deutero-Isaiah. He has reinterpreted the following motifs eschatologically: (a) the promises to the fathers (49:19–21; 54:1–3; cf. Genesis 28:11); (b) the deliverance from Egypt (52:12; cf. Exodus 13:21–2); (c) the journey through the wilderness (48:21; cf. Exodus 17-2-7) including the promise for the renewal of the covenant (55:3; cf. Exodus 24:11); (d) the re-entry into the Promised Land (49:8, 52:1).[25]

H. Hummel's ideas on 'typical thinking' in the Old Testament allow us to summarize various aspects of typology.[26] He writes that typical thinking is a dominant concern of the Old Testament, especially in its historiography, cultus and prophecy. Hummel distinguishes various elements of typical thinking. The first is the typical selection of the historical events. The Exodus and the twelve tribes, for example, are theological types. Secondly, there are typical individuals such as Abraham or Moses, the prophet *par excellence*. Aaron is the type of the priest and David is that of king. Thirdly, there are typical groups, for example 'the righteous versus the wicked' in the Psalms. A subdivision of 'the righteous' is 'the righteous sufferer'. Fourthly, there are typical nations: the very name of Israel has had an eschatological quality from the very beginning; Babylon and Edom have become transhistorical symbols of eschatological judgement. Fifthly, there are some typical individuals who stand for foreign nations, for example Gog and Magog. Sixthly, there are typical places such as Jerusalem and Zion. Some passages in Ezekiel (40–48) also suggest that the earthly temple is a 'type', a prophecy of the eschatological restoration of the entire cosmos.

Seventhly, those events that are not understood as being historical in modern terms but in the Bible they are seen as real or historical (for example the creation, the Garden of Eden, the

Flood, the story of Jonah), should be interpreted also as typical. The eighth element is very significant: Israel's cult is the best evidence of her typical thinking. In this cult 'the great redemptive acts of God were re-enacted or represented in a great theophany of renewed contemporization and confrontation, climaxing in covenant renewal'.[27] It meant always a recapitulation and actualization of God's never changing divine purpose. The cult signified not only a vertical unity of man and God but also a 'horizontal homology' of the past, the present and the future. Leviticus 16, as other writers maintain, can also be seen as a typological prefiguration of Christ's redemptive activity.[28] The New Testament, especially the author of the Epistle to the Hebrews, will take up the theme of this typological relationship.

TYPOLOGY IN THE NEW TESTAMENT

'The Scripture Fulfilled'

According to Frye's 'sevenfold phases of revelation' the whole Old Testament is 'summed up' in the discourse of prophecy and so it is the antitype of all the previous phases. But each antitype, we have seen, becomes a type of the following phase. It is then the claim of the Christian Bible that prophecy is fulfilled in the Gospel.

We read more than once in the New Testament that 'Scripture is fulfilled: *peplerotai he graphe* (Luke 4:21; Mark 15:28). It means that the text of the Old Testament was seen as being 'filled up' with power, that it was in the light of the gospel relevant and creative yet again. The logic of typology did not simply imply that the past was interpreted or reinterpreted but that this past was actually generating a new meaning again. The new eschatological event in history, that is, the 'Christ-event' sums up and fulfils previous history. Therefore the New Testament is the fulfilment or the antitype of the Old. Christ is the great 'recapitulator' who fulfils both the vocation of Israel and the will of God. However, the vocation of Israel was seen by St Paul as the vocation of mankind and therefore Christ fulfils not only Israel's history but all human history as well (Ephesians 1:10). The mystery of the Incarnation is that Christ identifies himself with the whole of mankind which, according to Charity, means that the history of mankind is implicit in the history of Christ.[29]

Christ Fulfilling the Figures in the Synoptic Gospels

We begin our reading of the New Testament with a look at how the authors of the synoptic gospels saw Jesus as fulfilling various typological figures.

The 'Prophet'

Within the pages of the synoptic gospels Jesus appears to his contemporaries first of all as a 'prophet'. Since he did not teach as the scribes did (Mark 1:22, 27) he was seen by the people as an Elijah or a John the Baptist *redivivus* (Mark 8:28; 6:14). The present *kairos* announced by Jesus (Mark 1:15) is also the fulfilment of the past. Jesus himself is the antitype of the Old Testament prophets. He is in the line of the prophetic tradition but he is nonetheless greater than they are. This is the motif of *Steigerung* which involves not only comparison but frequently an antithesis as well. Jesus has consciously fulfilled the figure of the prophet by preaching repentance: his words echo Jeremiah (Mark 11:17; cf. Jeremiah 7:11) or Isaiah (Mark 7:6; cf. Isaiah 7:11). 'Jesus, like the prophets, smashes the human ordinances and restores God's commandment.'[30] The Sermon on the Mount is a good example of typological logic. Jesus interprets the old by giving it new significance: he has not come to destroy but to fulfil the law. He is indeed portrayed as a new Moses but his phrase 'but I tell you' signifies the arrival of a new divine order.[31] He speaks with the voice of divine authority. Like the prophets in the Old Testament he did not simply castigate the sins of the people but proclaimed salvation both in word and in deed. He frequently borrowed expressions from the Old Testament to demonstrate that he was fulfilling it. Several of his miracles have parallels in the Old Testament: for example the cleansing of the lepers (Mark 1:40–45; cf. Numbers 12:10ff.; 2 Kings 5:1 ff.) or the raising of the dead (Luke 7:11–17; cf. 1 Kings 17:17ff.; 2 Kings 4:18ff); or the story of the miraculous feeding (Mark 6:35–43 par.; cf. Exodus 16:4, 1 Kings 17:8–16; 2 Kings 4:1–7, 42–44). Of course, not all the parallels are typological ones. There is frequently an Old Testament precedent for the manner in which Jesus exercises his authority. Jesus' encounter with the Canaaite woman (Mark 7:24–30 par.) for example is similar to Elijah's encounter with the widow of Zarephath (1 Kings 17:8–24; cf. 2 Kings 4:18–37).

Clearly, Jesus's death too is conceived within a typological framework by the synoptic writers. Jesus did not fall victim to his enemies. He taught about the necessity of his death during his ministry. Jesus fulfils the destiny of the prophets just as his enemies also 'fill up the measure of their fathers' (Matthew 23:32). This is well illustrated by the parable of the wicked tenants (Mark 12:1–12). Other Old Testament metaphors such as for example the 'rejected stone' (Psalm 118:22ff.; cf. Mark 12:10) or the 'vineyard' (Isaiah 5:1ff.) in the mouth of Jesus indicate that he was consciously evoking well-known images when he alluded to his death. Jesus was consciously expecting that he would die in Jerusalem (Matthew 23:37–39 par.; Luke 13:33; cf. 9:31, 51, 53; 18:31, Matthew 16:21). When the Jews demanded a sign from him, he referred them to the sign of Jonah: 'For as Jonah was three days and three nights in the whale's belly; so shall the son of man be three days and three nights in the heart of the earth' (Matthew 12:39–40 par.). In Matthew 16:4 Jesus explicitly speaks about the 'sign' (*semeion*) of Jonah.

The 'King'

Perhaps we may say that in the synoptic gospels Jesus viewed his whole life also as a fulfilment of the promises concerning the 'Son of David' and therefore that he 'fills up' the figure of the 'King'. This is most evident in the Gospel of Matthew which stresses the fact that Jesus was the descendant of David. But the genealogy shows that he is more than David because he is also the son of Abraham. Jesus the Messiah comes as David *redivivus*. That is implied in the allusion to David in the Sabbath controversy in Mark 2:23–28. If David the righteous king could eat the sacred bread on the Sabbath-day then he, the 'Lord also of the sabbath' (v. 28) may permit his disciples to pick grain on the Sabbath-day. It is reported by all four evangelists that Jesus so ordered his last entrance to Jerusalem that all people should recognize that the promise in Zechariah 9:9 was being fulfilled (Matthew 21:2ff. par.). Moreover, his anointing at Bethany (Mark 14:3–9 par.) was similarly the symbolic anointing of a King. Goppelt finds that even the shepherd metaphor from the Zechariah prophecy: 'smite the shepherd, and the sheep will be scattered' (13:7) falls also within the scope of royal typology because the shepherd is only a figurative title of the king.[32] Jesus had been at work on building the 'kingdom' from the very beginning of his ministry. The overall royal typology suggests that Jesus fulfilled both the figures of the Davidic kingdom and of the vocation of Israel.

The 'Son of Man'

Another figure that Jesus seems to be consciously fulfilling is that of the Son of Man. This expression is used as a title for Jesus about seventy times in the synoptic gospels and twelve times in the Gospel of John.[33] The title may simply mean 'human being' but when used by Jesus it has a special messianic flavour. The expression *bar-nesha* is mentioned in the Book of Daniel (7:13) which, according to Josephus, was much quoted by the Jews in New Testament times.[34] Though the figure of the 'Son of Man' in Daniel is sketched only very briefly, he is given unequalled authority and power over men and women at that future time when he is to make his appearance. This figure can also be found in the apocryphal Book of Enoch (1:37–71) and also in 4 Ezra. In Daniel the figure of the Son of Man is very close to that of the 'Ancient of Days' (7:9) sitting on a throne and pronouncing judgement. This activity in the Gospels is attributed to the Son of Man (Matthew 25:31; 16:27 and so on). The title may both conceal and reveal that Jesus himself is God in human form (cf. Matthew 16:13, 17). And it implies that he is seen to be also one of us – he is our brother. He is not just an ordinary man, but he is *the* 'Man'.[35] Jesus emphasized throughout his ministry that the Son of Man had to suffer and die. By his allusion to the suffering, however, Jesus combined, or fused, the Messianic figure of the Son of Man with the figure of the Suffering Servant of Deutero-Isaiah.

The 'Suffering Servant'

In Deutero-Isaiah there are four *Ebed Jahve* songs (42:1–4; 49:1–6; 504–9; 52:13–53:12) which present the figure of the 'Suffering Servant' (sometimes called the 'Righteous Sufferer' or the 'Servant of God').This is another figure fulfilled by Jesus in the New Testament. It is uncertain whether the shadowy figure in Deutero-Isaiah refers to one man or a pious remnant or perhaps even to a whole nation. Scholars are still debating whether it stands for an historical personality (perhaps the author himself?) or for a corporate personality (Israel?). To demonstrate that Jesus fulfilled this image, Goppelt reads the passion narratives in the context of their Old Testament quotations. The story of the passion is constantly being interpreted by the writers of the Gospels as fulfilment of Old Testament passages. There are dozens of passages from the Psalms (especially Psalm 22!) or from Jeremiah apart from those passages that identify the suffering Christ with the Suffering Servant. Describing how Jesus is mocked and ill-treated after the trial before the Sanhedrin in Mark 14:65 the author seems to have had Isaiah 50:6 in mind: 'I gave my back to the smiters and my cheeks to them that plucked off the hair: I hid not my face from shame and spitting.' And Isaiah 53:12 is seen to have been fulfilled by the fact that Christ is crucified between two criminals.

Matthew, however, identifies Jesus directly with the suffering servant using a quotation from Isaiah 42–1 to describe his earthly ministry:

> That it might be fulfilled which was spoken by Esaias the prophet saying, Behold my servant, whom I have chosen; my beloved, in whom my soul is well pleased: I will put my spirit upon him, and he shall shew judgement to the Gentiles. He shall not strive, nor cry; neither shall any man hear his voice in the streets. A bruised reed shall he not break, and smoking flax shall he not quench, till he send forth judgement unto victory. And in his name shall the Gentiles trust. (Matthew 12:17–21)

Whilst the servant is weak, despised and rejected, he is at the same time and paradoxically a mighty and a victorious conqueror who is taking vengeance on the nations and restoring Israel. In Isaiah's prophecy it is clear that the ministry of the servant is directed first towards Israel and only afterwards towards the Gentiles.

It is clear from these few verses that for the first Christians the figure of the 'Servant of God' was 'filled in' by Christ. Isaiah 53:11b has special significance: 'by his knowledge shall my righteous servant justify many, for he shall bear their iniquities.' The idea of the 'one for the many' is echoed throughout the Gospels (Mark 10:45,14:24 par.). This is the key to the idea of the forgiveness of sins.[36] Goppelt writes: 'Jesus' suffering, death and resurrection on behalf of 'many', that is, on behalf of all, accomplished what the self-surrender of all the martyrs of the Old Covenant could not do – the creation of a new people that has been sanctified by God and that will live forever.'[37]

In his brilliant phenomenological analysis of the *Ebed Jahve* figure, Paul Ricoeur shows that Christ's uniqueness consisted in his *combination* (or 'fusion') of the glorious figure of the 'Son of Man' with the pitiful figure of the 'Suffering Servant'. It implies that the way to a theology of glory leads through a theology of the cross. The image of the 'Judge', associated with the 'Son of Man' figure, is now connected with the sufferings of the servant. Hereafter the Son of Man is not only a 'Judge' but also a 'Paraclete' (Comforter, Advocate) and also a 'Witness'. Above all, and perhaps most unexpectedly, he also fulfils the role of the substitute 'Victim' in this cosmic trial. Satan remains alone, the 'Accuser' of the trial, his enemy Christ uniting the figures of the judge, the paraclete, the witness and even the victim. The Son of Man (who is also a King) is now identical with the suffering servant who is carrying the iniquities of many. The King had to become the victim: this is the mystery of Jesus.[38]

'Twelve Tribes – Twelve Disciples'

The church of Jesus can be interpreted typologically as well. Jesus appointed twelve disciples (Mark 3:14 cf. Luke 6:13; Matthew 10:1) clearly making an allusion to the twelve tribes of Israel. In the same way as God, Jesus also calls twelve followers who would represent the nucleus of a growing community. But the twelve disciples are not merely antitypes of the twelve tribes of Israel, they are themselves the types of an eschatological reality. Jesus is the corner-stone, the apostles the foundation-stones (Ephesians 2:20). In New Jerusalem the twelve gates bear the names of the twelve tribes of Israel (Revelations 21:12–24). Christ promises the twelve to share in his glory (Matthew 19:28).

The 'Passover' – The 'Last Supper'

The next important typological antitype in the Synoptic Gospels is the institution of the Lord's Supper. It is the Passover Feast in which the people of God celebrated their deliverance from Egypt. In Luke the Last Supper is referred to explicitly as the Passover meal (22:15). According to the writers of the Synoptic Gospels the Last Supper takes place during the night which corresponds to the eve of the Exodus of the children of Israel from Egypt when they were given particular instructions as to what and how to eat. (Exodus 12:8).

The reasons for sharing the bread and passing the cup also have their antecedents. The significance of the cup is that it refers to a covenant sealed with blood. It is unclear whether this is the blood of the Passover-lamb or the sprinkling of blood to seal the covenant at Sinai. However, the phrase: *haima tes diathekes* (Luke 22:20) is in verbal agreement with the Septuagint version of Exodus 24:8[39] suggesting more the analogy with the covenant at Sinai. From the interpretation in Hebrews, we can infer that as the old covenant was sealed with blood at Sinai, the covenant is also established with the blood of Christ. (Hebrews 9:18ff). Although if we were to take 1 Corinthians 5:7 into consideration we may perhaps conclude that the allusion is to the Passover lamb. Once again, the Old Testament types are 'fused' in the antitype of Christ's blood. Goppelt writes, 'that these two are inseparable and pulsate together in the words of institution, but, of course, without this clear conceptual definition of terms.'[40]

But we should bear in mind that the Last Supper is not only the antitype of the Passover; it is also a type in itself as well: the type of the great eschatological banquet (Luke 22:15–18 par.). Therefore the Lord's Supper always points to the eschaton, the consummation of time and history (Revelations 21:2 ff). Here we have to do again with the same kind of *Steigerung* as in the case of the twelve tribes and the twelve disciples. Jesus not only fulfils the types but lifts them up to a higher plane of reality.

The 'Lamb' and the New Creation (Typology in St John's Gospel)

Typology is also evident in the fourth gospel but it is very different from that in the synoptic gospels. Here Jesus is not simply compared to the Old Testament persons or figures but, as Goppelt argues, 'the basic orientation of this Gospel accounts for the fact that Jesus' work moves exclusively on the level of creation-typology'.[41] Accordingly, typology appears in two categories: firstly, Jesus is the Perfector of Creation, and secondly Jesus is the Perfect Gift of God.

The prologue (1:1–18) is a unique example of creation-typology. Only the Word was in the beginning and everything was created by the Word. The prologue announces that a new age has begun. 'In Jesus the redemptive gifts of the former salvation time come in perfected form, and this signifies that the first creation is being perfected in a new one.'[42] Even the idea of the 'new birth' (3:1–21) is basically a typological one as it can be understood on the basis of creation-typology: the new birth is, in fact, the renewing of the creation. But in order to make this new birth possible for the believer, the Son must be lifted up to the Father just as Moses lifted up the snake in the wilderness (3:14). Jesus can create everything anew because he perfectly fulfils the redemptive history of God.

Jesus as the perfect gift of God fulfils both the gifts of the first age of salvation and also the institutions of the Old Testament. The manna or the water pouring out from the rock were the gifts of God of the first age but Jesus gives the true bread from heaven. He is the bread of life (6:35; 6:48). And instead of mere water he offers 'living water': 'he that believes in me shall never thirst' (6:35b; 7:37–38).

The most perfect gift of creation is the Lamb itself, as it is the Lamb, this innocent animal, which perfects creation. John the Baptist's metaphor evokes the Old Testament institution of the sacrifice. Where does the symbol of the 'Lamb' ultimately derive from? Three suggestions are usually offered: (1) it may refer to sin-offerings in general. Two lambs were offered in the temple as part of the daily ritual-sacrifice (cf. Numbers 28:3f); (2) the servant of the Lord in Isaiah 53:7 is compared to a lamb; (3) Paul explicitly identifies Jesus with the passover-lamb in 1 Corinthians 5:7. John seems to imply that Jesus 'took up' the sins of many on himself and then he 'took it away'. In Goppelt's opinion, John has either the daily sacrifices or the passover lamb in mind. But it is likely that John's Gospel was written at a period when daily sacrifices had ceased to be performed, in which case the author would most probably have had a comparison of Jesus with the passover lamb in mind. And indeed this lamb was seen as delivering from death and destruction by the atoning power of its death (Exodus 12:7; 13:22). Whilst according to the synoptics Jesus celebrated this meal with his disciples on the evening before the Passover, in John it was celebrated 'at the hour specified by the law for the slaughtering of the Passover – lamb' (18:28; 19:14, 31).[43] This is reinforced in verses 19:33 and 36 when John records that Jesus' legs were not broken 'that the scripture should be fulfilled'. What John saw to have been fulfilled concerned the regulations of the preparation of the passover lamb ('neither shall ye break a bone thereof') in Exodus 12:46. This conception is in complete accordance with Paul's notion that 'Christ our passover is sacrificed for us' (1 Corinthians 5:7). From all this evidence it can be inferred that John viewed the Lord's Supper as the antitype of the Passover.[44]

Typology in Stephen's Narrative: Acts 7: 2–60.

Explicit typological structure is most strikingly illustrated in the speech of Stephen, the first Christian martyr, in Acts 7:2–60. This piece is a wonderful combination of salvation history and typology. Stephen begins the story of Israel by reciting the story how Abraham as the Patriarch was given the covenant of circumcision (7:8). Then he briefly mentions Isaac, Jacob and the twelve patriarchs, dwelling at length on Joseph (9–19). The longest section deals with Moses (20–44), and then Joshua (45), David (46) and Solomon are mentioned. So far the the audience can see no 'scandalous' element in this speech as up to this point Stephen evokes only their own history.

The reversal or the *peripeteia* of this monologue begins in verse 48 where Stephen quotes the prophet Isaiah (66:1ff.) and immediately applies this prophecy to his audience. In verse 51 he is already directly castigating the 'stiffnecked' (Deutoronomy 9:6) people who are 'uncircumscribed in heart and and ears' and 'resist the Holy Ghost'. This is a clear example of direct typology. By suggesting that their 'fathers' (this relationship is to be understood 'spiritually' rather than a 'carnally') persecuted the prophets, Stephen identifies his audience with the enemies of God and of the Just One of whom they 'have been now the betrayers and murderers' (52b). Stephen clearly implies that as Christ fulfilled the figure of the prophet, his audience, the enemies of Christ, 'subfulfill' (Charity's phrase) the figures of the prophets' murderers. When the high priests and the members of the council have heard this, the author of the Acts tells us, they were not simply offended but 'they were cut to the heart, and they gnashed on him with their teeth' (54) taking and stoning him there and then. In this they were re-enacting the role of the mob at the crucifixion, thus fulfilling both the figures of the enemies of the prophets and the enemies of Christ. Stephen, on the other hand, becomes identified with Christ; his last words: 'Lord, lay not this sin to their charge' (60) so reminiscent of the words of the crucified Christ: 'Father, forgive them; for they know not what they do.' (Luke 23:34). Significantly, these words are recorded only in the gospel of Luke which together with the book of Acts is usually accepted as the work of a single author.

There are, of course, a great many other elements of both vertical and horizontal typology in this speech. There is a reference to Moses who was to make the 'tabernacle of witness' according to the 'fashion' (or 'pattern') that is *typos* of what he had seen on the mountain (7:44; cf. Exodus 25:40). Horizontal typology is evident in references in verse 45 to Joshua (in Greek *Iesu*) who led Israel to the promised land which has been seen as a prefiguration of Jesus' redemptive activity. Even Joseph, one of the Patriarchs, can be seen as a type of Jesus. As he was sold by his brothers so was Jesus sold by one of his disciples. The allusion to the circumcision, first in the literal sense (7:8) and then by transference to a figurative sense (7:52), is also a sign of typological thinking in the context of prophecy and fulfilment. M. D. Goulder finds that even the Genesis-passages of Stephen's apology tell the story 'not just of Jewish hard-heartedness and perfidy, and of divine interdependence, but of the life of Christ, incarnate and in his church, foreshadowed in the scriptures of old'.[45] We can conclude that Stephen's apology is pervaded by typological thinking; it is indeed a miniature representative sample of an overall spirit of typology and salvation history that permeates the whole Bible and, indeed, is like a 'Bible condensed'.

The 'Old' and the 'New' (Typology in St Paul)

The American Old Testament scholar, E. Earle Ellis maintains that Pauline typology derives chiefly from three Old Testament periods: the Creation, the Age of the Patriarchs, and the Exodus.[46] Ellis distinguishes two basic patterns: 'the adamic or creation-typology' and 'the covenant typology'.

'Adam' (The Old and the New)

The Adamic or creation-typology is undoubtedly the most significant in St Paul's epistles. It is unparalleled in the New Testament because Adam is never mentioned in the Gospels. The most famous passage is at Romans 5:14 where Adam is described as a 'figure of him that was to come' (*typos tu mellontos*). Christ is not simply a 'Second Adam' or a 'New Adam', he is *the man*. He 'fills in' the figure of man, by his obedience he perfects the status of man.

It is important to see the whole context (5:12–21) because Paul's comparison of Adam and Christ involves both parallelism (5:12; 18ff.) and antithesis (15–17). Goppelt writes:

> In their acts and in the effects they have on others, Adam and Christ are related to one-another as a photographic negative to its positive print or as a mould to the plastic shaped by it. As the mould determines the shape of the casting, so from Adam's power over the human race comes Christ's mission and work, his death and his resurrection.[47]

The significance of this typology is that in Christ the Christian becomes a new creation. In chapter 6 Paul describes how by our baptismal immersion we die with Christ: our old self is crucified with him (6:6) and as we emerge from water in unity with Christ we become one with him in his resurrection (6:5, 9). Thus in our baptism we gain new life (6:4). Therefore, as he puts it in: 'if any man be in Christ, he is a new creature' (2 Corinthians 5:17). Christ fulfills the figure of 'Man' (Adam), therefore whoever is in Christ is also conformed with the God-designed model of 'Man'. The term 'to be in Christ' corresponds to the notion of 'to put on Christ' (Galatians 3:27), an image evoking a 'clothing-metaphor' so prominent throughout the Bible. Mankind that was 'in Adam' is now recreated 'in Christ' (1 Corinthians 15:22). 'The first and the second Adam are the progenitors of two races of men. Each implies a whole world, an order of life and death. Each includes his adherence in and under himself'.[48] Thus the Church is also a new creation and whoever is in Christ, belongs to the 'body of Christ' (1 Corinthians 12:27).

The 'Covenants' (The Old and the New)

Paul distinguishes two kinds of 'covenants' in his typology: the Patriarchal Covenant and the Exodus Covenant. Both are seen as types of the 'New Covenant', but the Abraham-covenant rather parallels, whilst the one at Sinai is as antithetical to, the new covenant.

Abraham and His Sons

We have seen that 'Abraham' was already the symbol of faithful obedience in the Old Testament. Jesus considered him also symbolically: Abraham is the father of all believers. Jesus chided those who regarded themselves the children of Abraham only on the basis of descendence, without reference to faith. Their 'father', Jesus said, was the devil (John 8:44). This suggests that in biblical language, 'sonship' or 'fathership' is to be understood in typological or spiritual terms, rather than in literal or 'carnal' terms.

Romans 4 is the *classicus locus* of Abraham-typology. Abraham believed only on the basis of God's given word and therefore, those who believe in Christ are the children of Abraham. Justification is not dependent on circumcision as this is only a seal received from God. Abraham was already a believer (and thus justified) while being uncircumscribed (4:12). The promise given to Abraham in Genesis 15:5 is fulfilled in his 'seed', that is, Christ (Galatians 3:16). Goppelt wrote:

> In the Bible, the terms – 'father' and 'children' (seed) – which describe a natural relationship defined by blood and by law become expressions for the interrelationship of type and antitype in redemptive history. In this relationship to God, Abraham is, in the fullest sense of the word, a type of all Christians in their relationship to God; consequently the promise of innumerable descendants that was made to Abraham is fulfilled in the gathering of the church.[49]

The other kind of covenant-typology perceives an antithesis between the covenant at Sinai and the covenant with Christ. In Galatians 4:21–31 they are related typologically to Abraham's two sons, Ishmael and Isaac, as we have seen it in the section on 'Primogeniture':

HAGAR + ISHMAEL	SARAH + ISAAC
SINAI (Moses)	JERUSALEM (Christ)
OLD COVENANT	NEW COVENANT

'Israel' (The Old and the New)

In our discussion of the Gospels we have seen that Jesus was seen to be the great recapitulator, the fulfilment of the history of Israel. Paul too has this presupposition in his mind. Typologically it is true that the 'believing Israel' is a type of Christ and the Church is the 'Israel of God'. Thus whatever happened to the Israelites, happened as 'examples' or 'warnings' (*typikos*) for the Church of

Christ which is now the people of God (1 Corinthians 10:6). If Christ was the 'perfected man', then the church is the 'perfected Israel'. When Paul says that 'they were all baptised unto Moses in cloud and in the sea' (1 Corinthians 10:2) he means that they were 'protected', 'enveloped' and saved by God just as we are protected, enveloped and saved by our baptism. The eating of the manna (Exodus 16:4:14–18) and the drinking from the Rock (Exodus 17:6; Numbers 20:7–13) are seen as types of the Lord's Supper (1 Corinthians 10:3ff.). These were gifts that preserved Israel in the wilderness just as the gifts of the sacraments are believed to preserve Christians today. The 'Rock' is also identified with Christ (1 Corinthians 10:4).[50] It is important to underline once again that the words *typos-typikos* have preserved an element of 'warning': these events or gifts are not only prefigurations but they are providential signs for the future, signposts of how, or how not, to behave in future analogous situations.

For Goppelt typology was the 'heart of Paul's theology':

> with Paul, typology is not a hermeneutical method to be used in a technical way to interpret the OT. It is a spiritual approach (*pneumatische Betrachtungsweise*) that reveals the connection ordained in God's redemptive plan between the relationship of God and man in the OT and that relationship in the NT.[51]

The 'High-Priest' (Epistle to the Hebrews)

It is not my intention to explore the depth and difficulty of the all-permeating typological theology of the Epistle to the Hebrews. I have chosen to concentrate on the central figure of the letter. In this epistle Christ is shown to have fulfilled another significant figure, almost as comprehensive as the figure of the 'Son of Man' in the synoptic gospels: the figure of the High Priest. Like the figure of the Son of Man, it involves humiliation and exaltation. This office was originally conferred upon the anointed one by God. As Aaron was called by God to be a high priest (5:4) so Christ was similarly chosen by God. The Psalmist's saying 'Thou art a priest for ever after the order of Melchizedek (110:4) is applied to him (5:6). This mysterious figure 'without father, without mother, without descent' (7:3) was seen to be greater than even Abraham since the father of all believers received blessings from him and even paid tithes to him (Genesis 14:20). Jesus' priesthood is thus superior to the Aaronic one partly because Jesus was not a descendent of the tribe of Levi, partly because his priesthood, unlike Levi's, is everlasting (7:23–25).

What then is the significance of Jesus' ministry as a high priest? Paul briefly alluded to Christ's atoning sacrifice in Romans 3:25. The theme is fully developed in this epistle. The Day of the Atonement is more explicitly evoked here. The Levitical high priest interceding for the people had to be both human and holy. He could attain holiness only by his daily sacrifices for his own sins. Christ is the perfect priest as he is both our brother and yet without sin (4:15). He does not need to bring any sacrifice for his own sin. In contrast to the Levitical priesthood, Christ does not need the earthly sanctuary as he has gone through the curtain which, according to the epistle, is his body (10:20) and thus opened for us a direct way to God. Matthew records that at the moment of Christ's death 'the veil of the temple was rent in twain from the top to the bottom' (Matthew 27:51). Thus the curtain separating the holy place from the holy of holies is taken away and a new way is opened for all believers. From now on, apart from Christ's intercession, no sacrifice or priesthood is necessary any more. Christ, the high priest, 'by his own blood . . . entered in once into the holy place, having obtained eternal redemption for us' (9:12) and since then he has been performing the service in the original heavenly tabernacle (9:11). It is the original *typos* of the earthly tabernacle that Moses was instructed to build (Exodus 25:40). In this case there is a hint of a vertical typology but it does not challenge the dominance of the horizontal typology, namely, that Christ is acting already in the advanced stage of salvation history.

Christ, the crucified one, performs his priestly service in the presence of God with his own blood. It means that Christ united the priestly and the prophetic concepts of the sacrifice ('fusion', again!): the former requires the shedding of blood and the latter the dedication of one's heart. By 'fusing' these traditions (just as he 'fused' the concepts of the Son of Man and the Suffering Servant) Jesus perfects the sacrifice. Fulfilling the type of his own sacrifice on the great Day of Atonement in Leviticus 16, Jesus too suffered 'outside the city-gate', that is by his crucifixion outside the city of Jerusalem. And Christians are, therefore, encouraged to go their own way 'outside the city' and separate themselves from the old Jewish dispensation. 'For here have we no continuing city, but we seek one to come' (13:14).

The tone of exhortation and warning permeates the whole epistle. As he unveils the new mysteries of redemption, the author addresses the believer and the church with passion, warning them not to fall into the Old Testament types (*hypodeigma*) of disobedience, by hardening their heart or losing their belief. At the same time he beseeches them to follow the figures or types of the true believers that are described in the celebrated eleventh chapter of the epistle.

The 'Stone' (1 Peter)

It seems entirely appropriate that an epistle which employs the stone-typology found throughout the Bible in such a concentrated form, should be attributed to Peter, whose name (*petros*, cf. Matthew 16:18) means 'little stone' and is closely related to *petra*, a 'rock'.

Turning then to the text of the epistle, we note that in the passage 2:4–8, the author speaks about the 'living stones' of the church. He quotes Isaiah 28:16: 'Behold, I lay in Zion for a foundation a stone, a precious corner-stone, a sure foundation: he that believeth shall not make haste.' Paul, as we have seen, has identified the foundation-stone with Christ (1 Corinthians 3:11). Peter's words – 'the stone which the builders disallowed the same is made the head of the corner' (2:7) – echoes those of the psalmist: 'the stone which the builders refused is become the head stone of the corner' (118:22). And perhaps there is too an allusion to the prophecy in the Book of Daniel concerning a stone that 'was cut out without hands, which smote the image upon his feet . . . and brake them to pieces' (2:34). In Matthew 21, Jesus evokes both the image of the rejected stone and the stone-image from Daniel and, once again, he is 'fusing' the two images. He applies them to himself and to the Jews thus announcing the advent of a new age in salvation history (Matthew 21:42–44). In Acts, Peter identifies the rejected stone with the head of the corner (4:11). For Paul, on the other hand, the smitten rock in the desert (Exodus 17:6) is identical with Christ (1 Corinthians 10:4). Thus 1 Peter combines various images of the 'rejected stone', the 'foundation stone', the 'stone of building', the 'stumbling stone', the 'rock of offence' and even the 'crushing stone'. This passage fuses various aspects of the stone as a symbol in salvation history and all the images are united in the one person of Christ.

Judgement – Typology (2 Peter and Jude)

Whilst in the Old Testament typology was characteristic rather of the 'weal'-prophecies than the 'woe'-prophecies, we can observe an opposite tendency towards the end of the New Testament: a new kind of typology is emerging in 2 Peter and Jude, and this is called 'judgement-typology'.

Judgement-typology is used to evoke the images of the fallen angels (2:4), the flood (2:5), Sodom and Gomorrha (2:6). There are two significant points here. First, all the Old Testament types refer to the future as not yet being fulfilled; second, the judgement always entails the salvation of the true believers who are saved in the midst of destruction.

In the Epistle of Jude (which is very similar in imagery and argument to second Peter) the author speaks of ungodly men who have crept into the congregations. They were 'before of old ordained to this condemnation' (4). The fallen angels (6), Sodom and Gomorrha (7), the 'way of Cain' (11), the 'error of Balaam (11), the 'gainsaying of Core' (11) are all types of those who will be judged in the future. Balaam also appears in 2 Peter 2:15 as the type of false teachers. He is the type of those who seduce others to idolatry because of greed. Sionce, in Numbers 16, Core rebelled against Moses and Aaron, Core is the type of those who rebel against the divine order. The non-canonical prophecy of Enoch is quoted to demonstrate that God will execute judgement upon the ungodly ones (14). These are said to be warning examples or patterns (*hypodeigma* in Peter 2:6 and *deigma* in Jude 7).

We can say that typology in 2 Peter and Jude is not directly applied to Christ (therefore the element of *Steigerung* is missing) but typology in these epistles refers to the future, to the judgement that is to come, the signs of which are already being felt and experienced in the present. This insight will be fully developed in the grandiose vision of the *Book of Revelation*.

THE LION AND THE LAMB (THE APOCALYPSE)

And I saw a strong angel proclaiming with a loud voice, Who is worthy to open the book, and to loose the seals thereof? And no man in heaven, nor in earth, neither under the earth, was able to open the book, neither to look thereon. And I wept much because no man was found worthy to open and to read the book, neither to look thereon.

And one of the elders saith unto me, Weep not, the Lion of the tribe of Juda, the Root of David, hath prevailed to open the book, and to loose the seven seals thereof.

And I beheld, and, lo, in the midst of the throne and of the four beasts, and in the midst of the elders, stood a Lamb as it had been slain, having seven horns and seven eyes, which are the seven spirits of God sent forth into all the earth.

And he came and took the book out of the right hand of him that sat upon the throne.   (5:2–7)

We have come to the Book of Revelation in our reading of Scripture. We seem to enter another world: the images, the sounds, the 'smells and the tastes' of this world are different. The experience is both surprizing and shocking. The colours of this book are unusually strong and dense, its music ranges in key and pitch. Our eyes are dazzled, our ears assaulted, our minds unsettled. Whence is this difference? Why is it that this book attracts the artists rather than the theologians? Why is it neglected in many Christian traditions and a closed book even for many who read their Bibles?

First of all, this book is a dense mosaic of allusion to the books of the Old Testament. Its text echoes Ezekiel, Daniel, Zechariah and Isaiah. If it is true to say that the language of the Bible is metaphorical rather than descriptive or argumentative then this claim is even more valid in the case of the Book of Revelation. There is even a *Steigerung* of this metaphorical language, if this German word really means a 'leap forward', 'like a shift of music into a new key as it crescendoes to a climax'. If earlier we have noticed frequent 'fusions' of motifs, here, we have arrived at a 'fusion of fusions'. Whilst we have become used to the metaphorical 'this is that' language in the Gospels: 'I am the vine, ye are the branches', we are perplexed by the innumerable floating metaphors in the last book of the Bible. In the Gospels the metaphors were relatively easy to understand: both the *tenor* ('I') and the *vehicle* ('vine') was stated. In the Apocalypse, however, we enter the world of 'implicit' metaphors, where the tenor is not stated. Similarly, this is the language of implicit types. We meet here metaphors of metaphors and types of types, metaphors, images, symbols, types 'floating', without 'legs', merging or fusing with one another. In this language there is no distinction between 'this' and 'that': this is a transparent language of identities without any argument. I use the word transparent in the sense of the *Oxford Dictionary*: 'Having the property of transmitting light, so as to render bodies lying beyond completely visible; that can be seen through.'[52]

One of the symbols around which this book revolves, is the 'book'. John of Patmos is told to 'write in a book' what he sees (1:11). In the text already quoted at length we have just read about the 'opening of the book', and in due course we shall discuss the meaning of the 'eating of the book' (10:9). Undoubtedly, the book's central concern is the 'Lamb's book of life' (21:27).

The passage (5:2–7) we have quoted above illustrates very well the nature and function of typology not only in this book but in the whole Bible. The Seer of Patmos has a vision of heaven. First he hears a resounding angelic voice asking: 'Who is worthy to open the book?' The mood is one of great solemnity and even dread. The question is not answered. There is only silence. The prophet is so distressed that there is no one worthy to open and read the book that he begins to weep. Then, suddenly, he hears the comforting words of one of the elders: 'Weep not . . . the Lion of the tribe of Juda, the Root of David, hath prevailed to open the book.'

There is twofold sense of surprize here. First, we are surprised and perhaps relieved that there is someone, still considered 'worthy' to open the book. Then, instead of the expected Lion of Juda, we are shocked by the prophet's vision of a Lamb 'as it had been slain' who comes, sits on the throne and opens the book, accompanied by the singing of the angels: 'Worthy is the Lamb that was slain, to receive power.'

In this condensed, poetic language there no logic or argument. It is intensive, paradoxical: the strong is the weak, the weak is the strong; whoever is dead might be alive and whoever thinks he is alive, might be dead. Those who consider themselves to be 'rich' are revealed to be 'miserable and poor' (3:17). The divine reality of the Apocalypse subverts all human sense of reality.

Within this divine vision the 'logical' human world becomes transparent and metaphorical. In this extremely dense, apocalyptic phase, language is highly revealing. It comes to us as a revelation that the Lion and the Lamb are one. The 'Lion', the powerful text of the Old Testament merges into the 'Lamb', the weaker text of the New Testament. But this 'interpenetration' of texts means that the Lamb becomes as powerful as the Lion, because *he* is the Lion. He is the reader, the recapitulator of the text, who identifies himself with the text and therefore, he *is* the text. The 'new' was concealed in the 'old', and now the 'old' reveals the 'new'. The seed has grown into a plant and the time of harvest has come.

We have seen the Lamb's reading of the book. Now, how does our 'reading' work in this specially intensified phase of language? To answer this question we turn to the intriguing image in 10:9, an echo, or 'intertext' of a passage in Ezekiel (3:1-3). The prophet is instructed to go to the the angel who stands with a little book, open in his hand. The voice tells him: 'take it, eat it up; it shall make thy belly bitter, but it shall be in thy mouth as sweet as honey.' We have undersood figure of 'swallowing up the book' as a metonym of appropriation, of how fulfilment is taking place. 'To swallow something up' is to absorb, assimilate, interpret, or, fulfill. Swallowing is incorporation or 'appropriation' in Ricoeur's sense of the word.

In the Bible each type is swallowed up or absorbed by its antitype but this does not mean that the type thereby loses its significance as happens in the case of allegory. Following Frye, we have described the Bible as a progress of types into antitypes within a scheme of the seven phases of revelation: creation is fulfilled (perfected) in the redemption of Israel in the Exodus. Exodus (or revoluton) points towards an intensified sense of law and the law is individualised (fulfilled) in wisdom. Wisdom looks for continuity and stability and therefore it widens out into to prophecy. For the Christian, the whole Old Testament is a prophecy, thus prophecy swallows up the whole Old Testament. In turn, the prophecy is swallowed up by the Gospel and the Gospel is eventually fulfilled in the Apocalypse. Is this the end? Does not the Apocalypse point beyond itself? Surely, it does. Does the Apocalypse also become an antitype? If so, of what is it the type?

If prophecy swallows up the Old Testament, we can say the Apocalypse sums up, fulfills or swallows up, the whole Bible. But if so, it must also become a type that points to something beyond it. Apocalypse is the type of the new creation, of a new heaven and a new earth. The Apocalypse lifts the Bible up into a new sense of reality, as it were into a higher key. 'The new Creation will actually incorporate the whole sequence; it would start certainly as a revolution in the reader's mind and would also encapsulate the whole sequence down to the apocalypse itself.'[53]

At the end of this reading we have arrived at the 'reader's mind'. But what happens to the reader, at the end of the day, when he has finished his reading of the Bible? We may say that the book is recreated in his mind: 'every text is a type of its on reading. Its antitype starts in the reader's mind . . .'[54] And the ultimate authority, according to Milton, is not the Book of the Bible but the Word of God in the human heart.[55] The purpose of reading is, indeed, to digest or 'eat up the book' and to be recreated by it. Here the Ricoeurian idea of 'appropriation' is indeed at work: if I 'eat' the book and 'swallow' the word, my ego will be extinguished, and I will become transparent. The reader is absorbed by the vision and recreated by it. 'The apocalypse', in Frye's words, 'is the way the world looks after the ego has disappeared.'[56]

4

Reading Pictures

VISUAL EXEGESIS: PICTURA QUASI SCRIPTURA

So we can now say that the end of writing is reading and reading is the recreation of the text in the reader's mind. The text is never written for its own sake, it is meant to produce an effect on the reader. The texts of Scripture were not written to be preserved or hidden away: these texts were meant *to be preached*. There is no record of Jesus commanding anyone to write the Gospel but there is a record of his command to teach all nations (Matthew 28:19). Therefore we can take the view that Scripture only serves to transmit an oral message or *kerygma*. This means, as Walter Ong[1] and others have frequently stressed, that orality precedes textuality. It is the oral voice, the 'living' voice coming from the 'mouth' of God, that is transmitted by the written words of the Bible. This voice as a 'double-edged sword' aims to reach the inner ear of the believer rather than to appeal to the eye. This may explain why the formula 'He that hath an ear, let him hear' is used with such a conspicuous frequency by Jesus in the Gospels. And also account for St Paul's classical formulation that 'faith cometh by hearing, and hearing by the word of God' (Romans 10:17). The texts are written to become *utterances* and they 'have meaning only in so far they emerge from and are converted into, the extratextual. All text is pretext',[2] says Walter Ong. The text is a medium to transmit the 'voice' from the 'mouth' to the 'ear'.

If we agree that the biblical text comes from a mouth and aims at the ear rather than the eye, then on what grounds can we account for, or justify the the highly visual nature of much Christian art? Is it possible to 'read' icons, Christian painting, sculpture or architecture as 'texts' being potential 'utterances'? Or, are they meant to be utterances at all? If not, to what do they appeal? What, for example, is a visual image? Is it a sort of mental picture, a projection of the mind? Undoubtedly, a visual image seems to strike or grasp the imagination more directly and immediately. But if seeing is more immediate, is it not more superficial? Can we trust our 'eyes' as much as our 'ears'?

This barrage of questions may be expressed differently as the problem of the relationship between the verbal and the visual. From time to time artists and scholars have wrestled with this problem, putting forward, for example, the old Horatian idea of *ut pictura poesis* which implies that the verbal and the visual arts are of the same root, because just as a poet is able to make his listener or reader 'see' an object, a painter is also able to make his forms and colours 'speak' to the beholder, who is thereby converted into a 'reader'. Intellectuals excited by these questions have turned to the disciplines of iconography and iconology. Indeed, iconology since the time of Cesare Ripa up to its modern rediscovery by Panofsky, Gombrich and their followers, has been based on the understanding that most visual arts can also be conceived of as texts to be both seen and read. Meaning is also inherent in the visual arts. Thus the visual arts can also be read as a special kind of symbolical language, where symbols are not meant simply to stir the imagination, but, as Paul Ricoeur has so often reminded us, are aimed at provoking thought.

Throughout the past twenty centuries of Christianity the proper attitude towards images or to the visual in general, has been a burning issue. We can observe two extreme positions at the limits of a wide range of attitudes: on the one hand there is the veneration or adoration of images, seen as 'idolatry' by less visually-minded people, and on the other hand, there is the attitude of iconoclasm often seen as barbarous and violent from the opposite end of the spectrum of view. Clifford Davidson speaks of 'The Anti-Visual Prejudice' and finds that the driving force behind iconoclasm, this 'religious phobia' is rooted in medieval thought about cognition and vision.[3] But we can find the origins of the iconoclastic impulses already in the Old Testament. The passage in Deutoronomy ('And ye shall overthrow their altars.') in 12:3 implies that the spirit of reformation has always been accompanied by the fervour of iconoclasm.[4]

The Struggle of the 'Ear' and the 'Eye': Some Manifestations of the Antivisual Prejudice

The anti-visual prejudice emerged very early in the development of Christianity, becoming manifest by the second century in a negative Christian attitude towards any 'spectacle', and particularly towards the theatre. This hostility towards the theatre is reflected in the writings of Tertullian and when the Puritans, almost fifteen hundred years later, attacked the theatre in England, these old anti-visual impulses came to the surface again.[5] The justification for this, frequently militant, Christian attitude could probably sound as follows: the 'eye' being attached to images becomes dependent on 'fixities' whereas God is always different from our fixities. God always challenges, even destroys, our images about him. But if we fail to recognize this un-ceasing divine activity and continue to adore *our* own fixed images of him, then we become the captives of our own imagination, the servants of *idols*. Therefore neither the sight of an image nor the 'vision' can be the source of illumination, they are simply illusions. Only the 'Word', received through hearing, can bring us to proper understanding.

Undoubtedly, the most famous outbreak of iconoclasm took place in Byzantine Christianity between 726 and 843. Both Art and Church historians have discussed this unique phenomenon intensively.[6] From our perspective, however, we need to focus upon the attitude towards to the visual in medieval Western Christianity and then on the reasons why this attitude was rejected by the radical representatives of the Reformation and, furthermore, how a moderate wing of the Reformation could eventually justify the existence of the arts, including the visual ones.

The veneration of images and sometimes even of relics in Christianity is well-known. Pope Gregory defended the significance of pictures in Christian life. He said that the images are introduced in the churches 'that those who are ignorant of letters may at least read by looking at the walls what they cannot read in books'.[7] In spite of the authoritative voice of tradition, the anti-visual prejudice occasionally became manifest even in the Catholic Middle Ages. For example, there was a debate about the use of images in Charlemagne's court in the twelfth century. The moderate outcome of the debate is reflected in the *Libri Carolini*.[8]

For all these local tensions the primary significance of the visual remained practically unchallenged throughout the Middle Ages. The average believer was meant to be satisfied with the 'sight' of *corpus dei* during the Eucharist and he was not invited to hear (or even understand) the word of God. Eusebius' old notion that 'the evidence of our eyes makes instruction through the ears unnecessary'[9] seems to have prevailed until the advent of the Reformation.

The Reformation radically reversed the medieval relationship of the 'eye' and the 'ear'. The reformers, with their discovery of the Word that comes from the mouth of God, stressed almost exclusively the significance of the divine voice appealing primarily to the ear of the believer. Luther turned Eusebius' dictum the other way round by saying that 'The ears are the only organs of a Christian'.[10] Elsewhere he said:

> A right faith goes right on with its eyes closed; it clings to God's Word; it follows that Word; it believes the Word.[11]

Margaret Miles, in her book *Image as Insight Visual Understanding in Western Christianity* (1985), informs us that the Reformation emphasis on hearing had been anticipated in the fourteenth century by Meister Eckhart who also recognized the priority of hearing over seeing. He associated hearing with a passivity which makes one able to to hear the voice of God. 'Seeing', he said, makes one's active faculties work. But these faculties themselves are sinful. Therefore, passivity, powerlessness are necessary if one is to hear the voice of a totally different being. Meister Eckhart said:

> Hearing brings more into a person, but seeing one gives out more, even in the very act of looking. And therefore we shall all be more blessed in eternal life by our power to hear than by our power to see. For the power to hear the eternal word is within me and the power to see will leave me; for hearing, I am passive, and seeing I am active. Our blessedness does not depend on the deeds we do but rather in our passiveness to God . . . God has set our blessedness in passivity.[12]

Luther and the reformers reaffirmed the significance of this passivity in listening to, and hearing, the Word of God. Passivity is necessary so that the activity of the Word could have its effect. Luther even saw the human language as a response to the Word of God and this language, he found, was born when one had pondered in one's heart the Word of God.[13] The following aphorism is attributed to Luther's followers:

Do not look for Christ with your eyes, but put your eyes in your ears . . . The Kingdom of Christ is a hearing Kingdom, not a seeing Kingdom.[14]

Luther's views about the significance of the ear and the dangers inherent in the eye were echoed later on by Donne, Milton and the English Puritans. Donne said that the eye was the 'devil's door', the portal of enticement and delusion. The eye was the most susceptable to demonic captivation.[15]

Luther articulated his anti-visual prejudice in his writings, but did not, like some of his radical followers, put his ideas into practice. A former colleague of Luther, named Karlstadt, however, published a pamphlet on the abolishing of images (*Von Abtuhung der Bilder*) in 1522. Karlstadt claimed that people are led astray by visual images which are the source of superstition and of idolatry. He confessed how deeply such images were rooted in his own heart and how they distracted him from hearing the Word of God.[16]

Margaret Miles describes with vivid detail how the removal of pictures and statues took place in Zwingli's parish-church, the Grossmunster in Zurich from 20 June to July 2, 1524 and how this became a 'model of iconoclasm in the Protestant territories of German-speaking Switzerland and Southern Germany.'[17] It is interesting to note that Zwingli himself was a great admirer of statues, paintings and images, and that he was a highly trained musician and composer. 'But aesthetic appreciation is not the same thing as conditioned attachment . . . Zwingli's support for iconoclasm came from his realization that images were to others what music was to him – an attraction so powerful that it irresistably drew attention from worship. '[18]

Luther's views on images, however, were not so fiercely iconoclastic as those of his radical followers. His attitude was more moderate and more civilized as well, and he once said that his own writings had 'done more to overthrow images than he (Karlstadt) ever will do with his storming and fanaticism.'[19] Luther discussed the subject of images and iconoclasm in the treatise *Against the Heavenly Prophets in the Matter of Images and Sacraments*. Here he wrote:

I approached the task of destroying images by first tearing them out of the heart through God's Word and making them worthless and despised.[20]

1. *Biblia Pauperum*:
   Magi (centre),
   Abner before David (left),
   Sheba before Solomon (right).

2. *Biblia Pauperum*.
    Egyptian Idols Fall (centre),
    Golden Calf (left),
    Dagon Falls (right).

3. *Biblia Pauperum*.
   The Jews Fall Back (centre),
   Foolish Girls Condemned (left),
   Fall of Angels (right).

4. *Speculum Humanæ Salvationis*.
Christ Prays for His Torturers,
Tubalcain and Jubal,
The Martyrdom of Isaias,
Moab Sacrifices his son.

He was convinced that the Karlstadtian manner of iconoclasm was 'to make the masses mad and foolish, and secretly to accustom them to revolution.'[21] Luther, on the contrary, admitted that his translation of the New Testament contained Cranach's woodcuts of the Apocalypse. He even designed a visual symbol of his faith, the so-called 'Luther-rose'.[22]

Luther approved and even encouraged the painting of biblical images on the walls:

> It is to be sure better to paint pictures on walls of how God created the world, how Noah built the ark, and whatever good stories there may be, than to paint shamelessly worldly things. Yes, would I to God that I could persuade the rich and mighty that they would permit the whole Bible to be painted on houses on the outside and inside, so that all can see it, that would be a Christian work![23]

The struggle between the ear and the eye seems to come to a stillpoint in the Lutheran Reformation. This moderate trend was not against art as such but it created a new foundation for the arts. The new spirit conceived a cleansed, purified art. This new-born, recreated art is manifested in the paintings of Dürer, Cranach or Grünewald, in the style of a new church-architecture and, above all, in the music of Johann Sebastian Bach.

'Visual Exegesis' and the 'Hermeneutics of Visual Images'

Having briefly glanced at some attitudes to visual images in Christianity and having looked closely at the Reformation outbreak of iconoclasm as a reaction to the medieval veneration of images, our theoretical conclusion must be that art, when it is not merely decoration or ornament, when it is not an expression of religious triumphalism, when it does not aim at seducing the eye but primarily, though gently and modestly, at transforming the mind, then we can, perhaps, consider visual documents as 'texts' which are meant to be 'read'. Moreover, in the Middle Ages visual images were frequently accompanied by written texts. As for the relationship between written and the visual texts, Miles has noticed three attitudes: (1) complementarity; (2) tension; (3) contradiction.[24] Using Miles' terminology, we may, perhaps, try apply a 'hermeneutics of visual images'.[25] True, images are unable to clarify a concept as subtly as words can do, but they also appeal to one's understanding and not merely to one's imagination. For Miles the claims of theological language and of religious images are complementary because they have:

> a similar structure for interpretation . . . both are inevitably interpreted on the basis of the perspectives, values, and interest of the interpreter.[26]

It is her conclusion that images just like language, should be powerful and 'therapeutic'. Images are idolatrous especially when they are subservient to commercial or political interests. But 'images belong to worship . . . Religion without artistic images is qualitatively impoverished; art without religion is in danger of triviality . . . '[27]

Besides Miles' 'hermeneutics of visual images' my second methodological pillar is the work of a Dutch medievalist, Anna C. Esmeijer who perceived some striking parallels between exegesis and art in the Middle Ages. It was she who introduced the fascinating term of 'visual exegesis', which means:

> a kind of exposition of Holy Scripture in which the customary roles of word and image have been reversed, so that the representation or programme provides the Scriptural exegesis in very compressed picture form.[28]

Esmeijer's pioneering and so far unique work encourages us to apply the methods of a visual exegesis in the 'reading' of some programmes of medieval typology. The idea of *Pictura Quasi Scriptura* suggests that pictures can elucidate Scripture just as Scripture can provide insights into pictures. With our typological vocabulary we can say that Scripture can also be fulfilled by pictures. The Scripture as a 'type' can find its 'antitype' in pictures. *Scriptura* is the 'figure' of *pictura* and thus *pictura* recreates *Scriptura*.

Esmeijer speaks about the didactic and mystical function of images, the latter going back to Platonic or Neoplatonic doctrines of mirroring.[29] Most of the examples we shall be discussing fall into the category of 'didactic' rather than 'mystical'. Unfortunately, for the twentieth century reader words like 'didactic' or 'schematic' have lost their original positive sense. Therefore, with the help of some apparently primitive illustrations we might be able to learn again what it originally meant to be didactic. For the medieval reader who had not yet lost the sense of their original interdependence, Scripture and picture were easily interchangeable.

In the following I shall analyse or 'read' several visual works of art with typological themes. I hope to show how these pictures, in their original and intelligent simplicity, are able to juxtapose Old Testament scenes with New Testament ones; how they are able to present sometimes unexpected, but convincing analogical patterns and correspondences. If *pictura* can be conceived of as a 'text', then these visual programmes will provide us with some excellent examples of intertextuality.

READING OF MEDIEVAL TYPOLOGICAL PROGRAMMES

It has been suggested by art-historians that Christian art has been typological in character from its earliest period, for example, on the walls of the catacombs and the early sarchophagi.[30] In the medieval period there are some outstanding visual 'texts' of typological character and it makes sense to concentrate on one or two examples in preference to a general survey. I propose to attempt some sort of 'visual exegesis' of these ultimately typological works. Such picture-books and cathedral windows do indeed interpret and, I hope to illustrate, even 'preach' the Gospel. But it would be naive to suppose that each artist was a pious and careful reader who converted his or her reading of the Bible directly into visual art. There must have been some mediating channels, some processes whereby the artist absorbed or learned the conventions of typology. The most obvious channel, of course, is the tradition of medieval exegesis or interpretation, and a great many insights, readings and misreadings of the Church Fathers were most probably heard from the pulpits of medieval churches. Isidore of Seville (560–630), for example, compiled a hermeneutical treatise *Allegoriae Quaedam Sacrae Scripturae*,[31] which could have served as a mediating channel. This work is a good example of a 'typological dictionary' though the author, of course, was not yet aware of the modern distinction between 'allegory' and 'typology'. Isidore enumerated some 129 names from the Old Testament, briefly mentioning what they prefigured. In the second part of the book the author discusses the figurative significance of several New Testament events, things and persons.

Another influence of the artist may have been the Church's liturgy, also derived in part from the Bible. For example, there is good evidence to claim that liturgy has had its impact on the compositional structure of the *Klosterneuburg Altar*.

A third type of channel or influence may be found in certain compendia compiled in the medieval period, containing correspondences between the Old and the New Testaments. And indeed, we know in most cases these works were compiled precisely for artists as aids and reference books for their works. There is also evidence that the artists indeed drew on these sources.

The *Pictor in Carmine* was one such medieval compendium. M. R. James called it a 'treatise', 'the largest known collection of types and antitypes intended to be used by artists'.[32] This work was probably compiled by an English cistercian monk at the end of the twelfth century. Several manuscripts have come down to us, out of which James could identify thirteen. The compilation contains 138 'chapters' which are, in fact, New Testament antitypes about Christ and his ministry. Each of these antitypes is correlated with other types, mainly from the Old Testament. The number of types related to each antitype ranges from two to more than twenty. Altogether there are 508 types listed.

The *Pictor in Carmine* consists of three parts: a Preface; the 138 'chapters' or concordance tables ('Tabula'); and in the third part the author 'gives us the distichs explanatory of the types, which make up the body of the book'.[33]

The tone of the Preface is highly personal. The author describes how he is horrified by 'foolish pictures' and 'misshapen monstrosities' he has seen in cathedrals and parish churches. But acknowledging the significance for the worshipper of the eye – the visual impact – he also recognizes how important the painter's choice of subject-matter can be. This reflection on the painters' responsibility, and on the use and abuse of images in churches, later found a distant echo in Luther's concessions to paintings in churches.

> I wished if possible to occupy the minds and the eye of the faithful in a more comely and useful fashion. For since the eyes of our contemporaries are apt to be caught by a pleasure that is not only vain, but even profane, and since I did not think it would be easy to do away altogether with the meaningless paintings in churches . . . , I think it an excusable concession that they should enjoy at least that class of pictures which, as being the books for

the laity, can suggest divine things to the unlearned, and stir up the learned to the love of those pictures . . . Therefore, it is that, to curb the licence of painters, or rather to influence their work in churches where paintings are permitted, my pen has drawn up certain application of events from the Old and New Testaments, with the addition in every case of a couple of verses which shortly explain the Old Testament subject and apply it to that of the New.[34] (M. R. James' translation)

Rota in medio rotae is the title of another compendium of typological correspondences probably complied in the thirteenth century and circulated in the region of Austria. The manuscript is sometimes called *Rota Ezechielis* or *Tabula Figurarum* or *Liber Figurarum*. As Floridus Röhrig pointed out, the *Rota* is in all probability a reworking of the *Pictor in Carmine* on a much smaller scale. It contains only 68 groups of antitypes with several types.[35] The most conspicuous difference between the *Pictor* and the *Rota* is, the absence of any images of the last things in the *Rota*.

The title of this compendium goes back to the famous and intriguing image of the 'wheel in the middle of a wheel' from Ezekiel 1:16. This special figure of Ezekiel's vision was frequently quoted in 'exegetical writings as an image of the concordance between the two testaments.'[36] The first writer to suggest this interpretation was probably St Jerome. It was certainly taken up by Pope Gregory the Great, Hrabanus Maurus and Bonaventura among others.[37] The Church Fathers, of course, read the Bible allegorically, finding this passage to be an expressive image of the organic unity of the two Testaments.

Röhrig's hypothesis is that the *Rota* was compiled, probably by Benedictines, in Southern Germany and Eastern Austria. And its main purpose, just as the intention of the *Biblia Pauperum*, was to defend the unity of the Old and the New Testaments against the sects of the Cathars who, emerging in the 12th century, denied the significance of the Old Testament altogether.[38]

THE KLOSTERNEUBURG ALTAR

One of the most famous and magnificent example of medieval typological art is an enamel altarpiece in the middle of the narrow Romanesque basilica of Klosterneuburg, near Vienna.[39] As it is recorded on the enamel itself, the *Klosterneuburg Altar* (henceforth: KA) was completed by the artist Nicholas of Verdun in 1181. The altar was revised and converted into a triptych by the addition of two groups in 1331.[40] The altar with its bright blue and golden colours appears even today 'like a glowing symbol of the salvation of God [incorporating] the two liturgical meanings of pietas as a central concept of the inscription: the merciful, redeeming love of God and his fascinating *tremendum*'.[41]

I shall be concerned primarily, with the typological features of this work of art 'reading', first of all its structure and design. Then I wish to say a few words about its possible theological sources and, finally, to pursue the question of the artist's identity.

The Structure

Nicholas Verdun's altarpiece, in each of its three sections, contains seventeen (a total of fifty-one) pictures depicting events in the Bible. Each picture and the whole work itself is accompanied by written inscriptions as well. In fact, there are at least four kinds of texts attached to the pictures. The longest one is the dedication-text that runs through the whole work, explaining its the purpose: 'to make the results of redemption plain, and awaken in men consciousness of grace'. Then each biblical picture is surrounded by a text containing the theme at the bottom and providing a short explanation in an inverted U-shape. Thirdly, there are short 'texts' appearing above and between the pictures of the second and the third rows. Fourthly, short but significant texts occasionally appear on the pictures themselves.

The work is designed to be read several ways. The pictures can be read both vertically and horizontally. The vertical reading of each coloumn (with the exception of the last two ones) reveals a typological correspondence. There is a horizontal structure in the central row which follows the life of Christ chronologically. In fact, the upper and the lower rows are not meant to be read chronologically. The altar was designed according to Augustine's famous three-fold division of salvation-history: *ante legem* (before the law); *sub lege* (under the law); *sub gratia* (under grace). The New Testament events (*sub gratia*) are placed in the central row (B) and they are flanked on either side by the Old Testament types: the upper row shows the events *ante legem* (A) and the lower row the events *sub lege* (C).

The following diagram will help us to understand the structure of composition:

	1	2	3	4	5	6	7	8	9	10	11	12	13	14	15	16	17
A																	
B									+								
C																	

| Infancy | Ministry | | Death & Resurrection | Church | Last Things |

+
Crucifixion

A = *ante legem* (OT types before the law)
B = *sub gratia* (NT events as antitypes)
C = *sub legem* (OT types under the law)

The central structural principle of the whole work is the horizontal chronology of the life of Christ in the middle row (B). Four groups are devoted to the infancy of Christ, four groups to his ministry (mainly the ministry preceding his death). The symmetrical mid-point of the whole composition is the crucifixion. It is followed by four episodes concerning Christ's death and resurrection. Two groups are about the beginning of the church (Ascension and Pentecost). Groups 16 and 17 depict the 'Last Things'. However, there is no typological correspondence within these two groups; the typological reading comes to an end in 15/C.

The very first image (1/A) depicting Abraham and the three angels contains a scroll with the inscription 'tres vidit et unum adoravit' (He saw three but adored only one). This inscription originally coming from Genesis 18:8 was earlier attributed to Augustine[42] but has been recently interpreted as an echo of the liturgy.[43] This picture and inscription at the very beginning of the work (1/A) comprise the symbolical nature of the whole composition: just as Abraham saw three angels and adored only one, the reader under grace is also presented with three images simultaneously (A,B,C) but they all point to the central one (B) which, as an antitype, fulfills, unites or integrates all in one. Perhaps the artist wanted imaginatively to grasp the mystery of the Trinity when he showed three in one.

TABLE 4.1 Scheme of the Klosterneuburg Altar

	(A) Ante legem	(B) Sub Gratia	(C) Sub Lege
1.	Promise of Isaac	Annunciation	Promise of Samson
2.	Birth of Isaac	Nativity	Birth of Samson
3.	Circumcision of Isaac	Circumcision of Isaac	Circumcision of Samson
4.	Abraham & Melchizedek	The Magi	Queen of Sheba
5.	The Exodus	The Baptism	Laver on 12 Oxen
6.	Moses goes to Egypt	The Entry	Paschal Lamb
7.	Melchizedek	The Last Supper	Manna in the Ark
8.	Death of Abel	Betrayal	Death of Abner
9.	Isaac Offered	Crucifixion	Spies and Grapes
10.	Eve's Fall	Deposition	King of Jericho Taken
11.	Joseph in the Pit	Burial	Jonah Swallowed
12.	First Born Smitten	Harrowing of Hell	Samson & Lion
13.	Jacob's Blessings	Resurrection	Samson & Gates
14.	Enoch Translated	Ascension	Elijah Taken Up
15.	Noah's Ark	Pentecost	Giving the Law
16.	Second Coming	Angels' Trumphets	Resurrection of the Dead
17.	Heavenly Jerusalem	Jesus Judges	Hell

Reading Pictures 91

It will probably be easier to understand the programme if we give the whole scheme a vertical twist (as in Table 4.1). If we look the altar in its original horizontal position again, we will notice that though each tripartite grouping is complete in itself, they are also related to the horizontal progress of salvation history, thus each picture is characterized by a tension of two diametrically opposite and opposing forces. Groseclose observed that the scenes of the composition are placed in an

> architectural setting which progresses as a continous arcade. An even more fundamental architectural principle may be recognized in the total disposition of the scenes in that this typological scene can, in this visual medium, be expressed as mathemathical and spatial values, i.e. the concept is two prefigurations per New Testament unit (roughly as a mathemathical ratio), and this concept is expressed through spatial placement of the prefigurations above and below the Christian event. In this manner the two organizing principles – typology and chronology – while actually running in opposite directions, are fused through architectural values. This solution allows development of the expressive and structural potentials of both typological fractionalization and narrative progression because each procedure complements the other in the total work.[44]

We have mentioned that 8/A-B-C and 10/A-B-C were only inserted two hundred years later after the original composition. Two New Testament scenes were added: the Betrayal and the Deposition, with their Old Testament prefigurations. From the choice of types it becomes obvious that the later artists were not really familiar with the nature of typology any more. The correspondence established between the New Testament scenes and their Old Testament antitypes, is rigid and formal, entirely lacking the vision of spiritual correspondence, that created cohesion in most of the other groups in the composition. Thus Judas' betrayal is seen to have been 'prefigured' by the murder of Abel by Cain and the murder of Abner by Joab. In this second case the author was evoking the story in 2 Samuel 3:27 but the correspondence he noticed was no more than superficial, as Abner could never be seen as figuring Christ. Similarly, the prefigurations of the 'Deposition' (10/B) are Eve's picking the apple from the forbidden tree (10/A) and the deposition of the King of Jericho (properly Ai) from the tree as it was recorded in Joshua 8:9 (10/C). The choices of the forbidden fruit and the body of Ai as 'types' of the dead body of Christ are grotesque and entirely inappropriate. These situations or actions are only vaguely similar to one another. Therefore the typological correspondence is arbitrary, artificial and formal, lacking any authentic inner cohesion. There is here no real intertextuality at work.

The centre of the whole symmetrical composition is the image of the crucifixion (9/B). The biblical text behind the central image is from Daniel 9:26: 'Post haec occidetur Christus' (And after three-score and two weeks shall Messiah be cut off.) The *ante legem* prefiguration is Abraham's sacrifice of Isaac showing with them the angel and the ram, the latter figure adumbrating the substitutionary nature of Christ's sacrifice. The *sub lege* prefiguration is the episode concerning the bunch of grapes which the spies brought back from the Promised Land. This symbol is very old in Christian art, going back to the earliest catacombs. The two poles carried by the spies signify the cross, the grapes hanging over the poles signify Christ, whose body is the true vine. The two spies looking at the grapes they carry signify the Old and the New Testaments. The one going in front looks back at the grapes. He represents the Old Testament. The one going behind looks ahead towards the grapes and follows the steps of Christ. He represents the New Testament.

The resurrection (13/B) is prefigured in Jacob's blessing of Judah, the 'lion' in Genesis 49:9 ('Who shall rouse him up?'). The sleeping lion is a prefiguration of Christ. It is interesting to see that the author, perhaps intentionally, has blurred the distinction between prophecy and typology. He was, in fact, echoing the tradition of the Fathers: 'Prophetia est typus in verbis, Typus est prophetia in rebus, in quantum res esse noscuntur.[45]

The Sources

In trying to track down the sources of the KA, we cannot relate it to such typological compendia into account as, for example, the *Pictor*, or the *Rota*, because these were composed, as we have seen, later than the altar. Recently, Helmut Buschhausen, a scholar working on the altar, suggested that the liturgy of the ecclesiastical year was the primary source or inspiration for the altar, especially for the middle row. And indeed, all the prophetical proverbs and the inscriptions in the middle row are seen to have been taken from the liturgy.[46]

Another important source of the altar, mentioned by Buschhausen, are typological sequences, the so-called *Zwischengesänge*, responsorial verses involving congregations in active participation which are in character typological rather than doxological. Such responsorials were composed at various Augustinian monasteries, mainly in Austria and Southern Germany. Some were composed by, for example, the monks belonging to the Victorine school in Paris. Adam of St Victor is said to have written such sequences. One of them begins as follows:

> Lex est umbra futurorum
> Christus finis promissorum
> Qui consummat omnia [47]

Buschhausen even maintained that the new sacramental views of Hugh of St Victor, the founder of the order, had significantly contributed to the formation of a principle by which the individual types were fitted into the larger scheme.

The Designer

From the inscription we know for sure that the altarpiece was the work of the artist, Nicholas Verdun. Artists usually relied on the works of knowledgable theologians. But who could have been the theologian directing the work? In Buschhausen's view it must have been Rudiger, the Dean of Klosterneuburg from 1165 till 1170 and its prior 1167–8. Clearly the motive behind the composition of this work was a need to defend traditional teaching against contemporary secularizing trends amongst the clergy.[48]

THE BIBLIA PAUPERUM

I have chosen the *Biblia Pauperum* (henceforth: *BP*) as a second example for my reading of medieval typological works. The *BP* is a book containing a series of pictures and texts based on the life of Christ. Each image from the New Testament is flanked by two Old Testament prefigurations. There are altogether twelve elements, three pictures and nine various texts, on each page. The *BP* was probably first compiled in the thirteenth century in South Germany.

The Aim and Structure

The basis of my discussion is Avril Henry's most learned and excellent recent edition of the *BP* (1987). Henry argues convincingly that the book was not meant simply for the 'poor' as its modern title would suggest, nor for children, nor even for the 'stupid' as suggested by some critics. But it was primarily intended for meditation and probably compiled orginally by a well-educated and learned theologian:

> The strongest argument for the book's being intended for meditation is perhaps the way in which the twelve elements on each page ... interrelate. It is hard for us to practice the concentration, the receptive sensitivity to image and word, which is required to perceive their patterns ... But the difficulty should not blind us to the fact that the educated medieval mind was more likely than the modern mind to be trained in image interpretation, in recognition and understanding of half-quoted biblical texts, and above all in the process of meditation which is the prelude to prayer.[49]

Among the three pictures on each page, the central one is from the New Testament and the other two are seen as Old Testament prefigurations of the New Testament scene. The three pictures are accompanied by various texts, always in the same order. The book follows the narrative of the New Testament, it begins with the Annunciation and ends with Christ's presenting the faithful the crown of life after the Last Judgement. The length of the cycle varies according to the individual manuscript, as does the number of the groups which ranges from 34 to 50. Avril Henry's edition presents 40 such groups: the first twenty (from 'a' to 'v') provide a survey from the Annunciation to the culmination of Christ's ministry with the appropriate prefigurations; the second half of the cycle (from '.a.' to '.v.') presents the New Testament events and their prefigurations from the Betrayal to the apocalyptic Crown of Eternal Life. The name for the collection *BP* has been used only since the eighteenth century, some other versions are called as *Concordance of the Old and the New Testaments*.[50]

The texts vary in length and style. On the top left and right hand sides of each page there are two *lectiones* that describe how the two types are related to the central antitype. Each page contains four prophecies (*versus*) above and below the pictures. Lastly, each of the three scenes has a rhyming caption (*titulus*). The two *lectiones*, the three *picturae*, the four *versus* and the three *tituli* make up the twelve elements on each page. The following diagram shows how they are related to one-another.

lectiones:	1, 2
versus:	3, 4, 10, 11 (prophecies)
picturae:	5, 6, 7 (the central NT event: 5)
tituli:	8, 9, 12

1	2
3	4
6 / 5 / 7	
8	9
10	11
12	

Avril Henry's facsimile edition is based on the Dresden and Chantilly impressions and it includes the transcriptions of all the Latin texts with their English translations and with a huge scholarly apparatus. Though it does not claim to be a 'critical edition', it nevertheless incorporates most of the information included in previous editions as well as offering both the transliteration of the Latin texts and their English translations.

On the basis of the 40 group facsimile, Henry has attempted to divide the whole cycle into ten thematic quartets which she calls 'chapters', finding that these scenes are often linked in terms of thematic design. For example, chapter 2 ('e') begins with the Holy Family moving from the left to the right and it ends with their return from the right to the left ('h').[51] The ten chapters are as follows:

1. Infancy (a–d)
2. Egypt (e–h)
3. Godhead manifest (n–q)
4. Kingship manifest (n–q)
5. Betrayal prepared (r–v)
----
6. Passion (.a.–.d.)
7. Death and Tomb (.e.–.h.)
8. Resurrection (.i.–.m.)
9. Church established (.n.–.q.)
10. Four Last Things (.r.–.v.)

The forty groups can be summarized in according to scheme laid out in Table 4.2 (on the following pages). With the help of this diagram we can easily recognize the provenance of the individual scenes. We can see immediately how purely 'biblical' the *BP* is. In the next section we shall study its successor, the *Speculum Humanae Salvationis* which enlarges the original of the *BP* by adding several extrabiblical scenes. We shall see that despite its claim to be a 'richer' compilation it has frequently lost the original gravity of its 'poorer' predecessor. In the *BP* most of the types are taken from the Old Testament: two types are taken from the New Testament (.m.7 and .v.7) and two are taken from the Deutero-canonical or Apochryphal books (p7 and .a.7). With the exception of two scenes (f5 and .q.5) all the antitypes are from the New Testament. The only two extrabiblical scenes concern the fall of the Egyptian idols (f5) and the coronation of the virgin (.q.5).

How is typology used in the *BP*? Henry distinguishes at least six kinds of relationship:[52] (1) simple parallels between externally similar events (as the killing of Abner prefigures the betrayal of Christ in .a.6). (2) Occasionally types are taken not from the Old

TABLE 4.2 Scheme of the Biblia Pauperum

a	Eve & Serpent	ANNUNCIATION	Gideon's Fleece
b	Moses & Burning Bush	NATIVITY	Aaron's Rod
c	Abner Before David	MAGI	Sheba Before Solomon
d	Law of Presentation	PRESENTATION	Anna Presents Samuel
e	Jacob Flees Esau	FLIGHT TO EGYPT	David Flees Saul
f	Golden Calf	EGYPTIAN IDOLS FALLS	Dagon Falls
g	Saul has Priests Slain	MASSACRE OF THE INNOCENTS	Athalia Slays Prince
h	David Returns	RETURN FROM EGYPT	Jacob Returns
i	Crossing the Red Sea	BAPTISM	Bunch of Grapes
k	Esau Sells Birthright	TEMPTATION	The Fall
l	Elias raises the Sarephtan	RAISING OF LAZARUS	Eliseus Raises the Sunamite
m	Abraham & 3 Angels	TRANSFIGURATION	Three Youths in Furnace
n	Nathan Brings David to Repentance	MARY MAGDALENE REPENTS	Miriam Repents
o	David is Greeted	ENTRY INTO JERUSALEM	Eliseus Greeted
p	Darius Purifies the Temple	CHRIST PURIFIES THE TEMPLE	Judas Machabeus Purifies the Temple
q	Conspiracy against Joseph	CONSPIRACY	Absolon Conspires against David
r	Joseph is Sold to Ismalites	JUDAS PAID	Joseph Sold to Putiphar
s	Melchisedech offers Bread & Wine	LAST SUPPER	Moses & the Manna
t	Micheas punished for Predicting Defeat	CHRIST PREDICTS HIS PASSION	Eliseus Condemned for Predicting Truth
v	Foolish Girls Condemned	JEWS FALL BACK	Fall of Angels

TABLE 4.2 Scheme of the Biblia Pauperum (Cont.)

a.	Joab Kills Abner	JUDAS BETRAYS CHRIST	Tryphon Betrays Jonathan
b.	Jezabel seeks Eliseus' Life	JEWS CONDEMN CHRIST	The King Condemns Daniel
c.	Noah's Nakedness Mocked	CHRIST MOCKED	Boys Mock Eliseus
d.	Abraham & Isaac	CHRIST CARRIES CROSS	Woman of Sarephta
e.	Abraham's Sacrifice	CRUCIFIXION	Brazen Serpent
f.	Eve Drawn from Adam	CHRIST PIERCED	Moses Strikes Rock
g.	Joseph in the Well	ENTOMBMENT	Jonas Swallowed
h.	David Kills Goliath	CHRIST OPENS LIMBO	Samson Kills Lion
i.	Samson & Gates of	RESURRECTION	Jonas Released Gaza
k.	Ruben at the Well	THREE WOMEN AT THE TOMB	Bride Seeks Beloved
l.	Daniel is Found	MARY MAGDALENE FINDS CHRIST	Bride Finds Beloved Among the Lions
m.	Joseph Reveals Himself	CHRIST APPEARS TO DISCIPLES	Return of the Prodigal Son
n.	Gideon & Angel	DOUBTING THOMAS	Jacob Wrestles with the Angel
o.	Henoch Ascends	ASCENSION	Eliseus receives Elijah's Mantle
p.	Moses Receives the Law	PENTECOST	Elijah's sacrifice is accepted
q.	Solomon Enthrones Bethsabe	CORONATION OF THE VIRGIN	Assureus Crowns Esther
r.	Judgement of Solomon	THE LAST JUDGEMENT	David Condemns the Amaeecite
s.	Dathan and Abrion are engulfed	THE DAMNED IN HELL	Sodom and Gomorha burn
t.	Job's Family Feasts	CHRIST GATHERS BLESSED SOULS	Jacob's Ladder
v.	The Groom Crowns the Bride	CHRIST GIVES THE CROWN OF ETERNAL LIFE	The Angel & St John

but from the New Testament (the foolish virgins of the parable prefigure the falling back of the Jews in v6, or, the return of the prodigal son is seen as a type of Christ's reappearance to his disciples after the resurrection in .m.7). (3) Sometimes the relationship between the New Testament scene and its type is puzzling. Why, for example, 'Gideon's Fleece' is to be seen as the type of the 'Annunciation' (a5, 7) or the 'Burning Bush' of the 'Nativity' (b5, 6)? The *lectiones*, based on some patristic sources, however, make the correspondences work. (4) The relationship may be causal: the 'Fall' is the cause of the 'Temptation' (k5, 7). (5) Some relationships refuse to be categorized as in .v.. (6) Most of the relationships are truly prefigurative ones. But within this last category one can make a further distinction as between (a) parallels: for example as Joseph was put into a well, Christ was similarly placed into the tomb; and (b) contrast: whilst Isaac did not die as a victim of the father's sacrifice, Christ did.

German scholars have tended to describe these relationships or analogies between the type and the antitype in term of various 'rhymes'. Thus one reads of 'symbol-rhyme' (for example, Gideon's Fleece – Mary's virginity); 'meaning-rhyme' (for example, the golden-calf and the apocryphal fall of idols) and, most frequently, 'situation-rhyme' (for example, the adoration of the magi as prefigured by the visit of the Queen of Sheba to Solomon.)[53]

What do we know about the earliest version of the *BP*? In spite of some speculation on the matter, nobody really knows who the original author was. The first copy, now lost, must have been made around 1250.[54] Most of the remaining manuscripts are in Latin. Meticulous German scholarhip distinguishes three manuscript families from (1) Austria; (2) Weimar and (3) Bavaria.[55] and some scholars suggest that a copy from the Austrian family could have been influential in the reworking of the Klosterneuburg altarpiece. Claims that the *BP* was composed and circulated as a defence against the emerging Manichean sects are, in Henry's view, unproven.[56] Clearly, however, the *BP* was extremely popular in the fourteenth and the fifteenth centuries. It was amongst the earliest printed books, and by 1460, was already in blockbook form with the pictures and the texts in woodcut.[57]

The *BP* was most probably intended primarily as a book for meditation with the purpose of strengthening faith. But we can surmise that it could also function as a manual for preachers. In fact, it would be quite easy to label each group with a title relating it to a particular topic: for example, 'homecoming' (h); 'greediness (w); 'the power of God (l) or 'repentance' (n); 'the fate of the prophets' (t); 'betrayal' (.a.); 'obedience' (.d.); 'power' (.i.); emptiness (.k.); 'recognition' (.m.); 'doubt' (.n.); 'the divine integration of the community' (.t.); 'the divine integration of the individual' (.v.). Those who used the book could always follow its guidance in the concrete problems of everyday life whilst preachers, perhaps, could use it for series of sermons or retreat or at a certain period in the ecclesiastical year, for example, during the forty days of Lent. Medieval man was fascinated by 'meditative objects' like the *BP* and his mind was trained to perceive the similar or analogical patterns occuring frequently in God's salvation history as presented to him in such a book. His training had also made him sensitive to the possibilities of the past being reactualized in the present.

Having tried to look at the totality of the composition, in concluding this introductory passage I am going to concentrate on three individual groups and through these selected readings I hope to show how the interplay between the visual and verbal elements generates meaning. In my analyses I am trying to imagine how a medieval priest could convert his reading of the individual groups into sermons. Reading the *BP* one feels that this interplay between the *pictura* and the *textura* has a special compelling rhetoric that almost asks to be expressed as a sermon. To demonstrate this I have selected three pictures for reading.

(1) The Adoration of the Magi (A Reading of Group 'c')

When exponding upon scene (c) [illustration 1], our imaginary preacher would not only recite this well-known epiphany-story but would also tell the stories suggested as prefigurations of the visit of the Magi. One of such episodes is the story of a former captain of King Saul who defected to the camp of David. The other episode is the story of the Queen of Sheba visiting the court of Solomon. What, then, is the common element in these three stories? One recognizes that they are not merely about 'visits'. The point is arguably that the elect person, whether David, Solomon or Christ, is *honoured* by someone who is from a *foreign* stock. Whilst Abner, the Queen of Sheba and the Magi could not claim to belong to God's people, they all recognized the divine authority of the elect one. So they did the most they could do: they venerated the elect one whether by joining him or by giving him presents. Isaiah's prophecy is quoted as a verbal support to the episodes: 'All nations shall flock to him' (2:2–3). The other prophecy is perhaps even more striking, for the Messianic prophecy 'A star should rise out of Jacob' (Numbers 24:17) is uttered by Balaam, the *foreign* prophet who did not belong to the people of Israel. Our preacher would probably stress throughout his sermon that although God always chooses a people of his own for his purposes, his power and majesty may also be revealed to those who are perhaps the farthest from the chosen ones. God's gradually unfolding rule is not exclusive. He is willing to adopt the stranger or even the strangest. That is why he opened the way for the Gentiles in his plan of redemption. Christ always accepts, even rewards those 'foreigners' who, in their search for truth set out on a spiritual pilgrimage to find him. He does not preclude the sincerity of those whose recognition of his divinity comes – strangely, unexpectedly – in a moment of revelation like the malefactor on Calvary whose sincere repentence was accepted by Jesus without conditions: 'Verily I say unto thee, To day shalt thou be with me in paradise' (Luke 23:43).

(2) The Fall of Idols (A Reading of Group 'f' [Illustration 2])

A sermon of an entirely different character could be based on the 'f' group of the *BP*, castigating the hypocritical religiosity of contemporary church-goers, in terms of an attack on idolatry and the veneration of foreign gods. The sermonizer would immediately recognize the harmony and concordance of the images and prophecies. Moses' smashing the golden calf is echoed in the image of the fall of Dagon, the god of the Philistines (1 Samuel 5:1–5). Just as the image of Dagon falls down when the Ark of God is placed next to it in the Philistine temple, so all the idols of Egypt collapse in the presence of the infant Christ, according to the eighth- and ninth-century legend later recorded by Peter Comestor in his *Historia Scholastica*. This is explained by the *lectiones*, illustrated by the pictures and confirmed by the prophecies: 'he shall break down their idols' (Hosea 10:2); 'Now I will destroy their every image in the house of your god' (Nahum 1:24); 'I shall eradicate the names of their idols from the earth' (Zechariah 13:2); 'The Lord will bring low all the gods of the earth (Sephaniah 2:11). Verbal and visual images, *textura* and *pictura* corroborate one-another once again. These apparently heterogeneous, unconnected elements are carefully composed and woven together like the powerful, harmonious music of an organ.

(3) The Jews Falling Back from Christ (A Reading of Group 'v' [Illustration 3])

A further sermon might be quarried from the fourth piece in the 'chapter' on Betrayal. It is located right at the end of the first half of the cycle (v). The central New Testament picture entitled 'The Jews Fall Back From Christ' depicts events shortly before Christ's Passion. We are in the Garden of Gethesemane. The guards seeking Christ, drop back and fall down when they hear Jesus saying: 'I am He' (John 18:6). They are overpowered physically by the revelation of his divinity. The significance of this moment is greater still. The tragic moment marks the symbolical, figurative falling back of the Jews: the loss of their privileged status as being the chosen people. The previous group of images in the cycle was concerned with the rejection of the prophets and the dismissal of the Son of God. This group of images takes us a step further, showing the consequences of this disobedience. The central message of the composition is that however close we may be to God, we may easily lose our privileges. However near to our God-intended destination we are, we may easily fall 'out of the way' if we slip or disobey. If we do not hold fast to God, the prospect of our 'exclusion' looms over our heads. As we have seen above, God can always easily graft foreign stock to his ever-growing 'tree of salvation' instead of useless, dry branches. Thus this group is an interesting counterpart of group 'c'. In spite of our uselessness he will accomplish his redeeming plan, as we have seen clearly in the first 'sermon'. This thesis is affirmed by both prefigurations or types. These types are taken from salvation history probably because the antitype itself was also a crucial event in that salvation history. We may find it extremely disturbing when the 'Fall of Angels', the story of Lucifer (Isaiah 14:12–5 and Revelation 13:9) is presented to us as the prefiguration of the fall of the Jews. The Jews, like the former angels have enjoyed a privileged status in the divine economy. Both of them fall tragically from this state of grace. However, the evocation of the New Testament parable of the foolish virgins (Matthew 25:1–13), the other prefiguration, supports the view that a type is not simply a past event because a parable can also function as a paradigmatic warning or 'exemplum' for the future, as if to say this might easily happen again, even among the followers of Christ. The bridegroom closes the gate, for the foolish virgins who do not have oil in their lamps are effectively excluded. The type is thus converted into prophecy: the foolish virgins, because of the deadness of their hearts, will 'fill up the measures' of both the fallen angels and of the fallen Jews.

All three images in the group deal with God's righteousness as radically different from the righteousness of men. This is made clear at the creation of the world (in the story of the fallen angels), just before the culmination of Christ's redemptive ministry (in the story of the fall of the Jews), and will be once again at the end of the world (as it is foretold by the prophetic parable of the foolish virgins).

THE SPECULUM HUMANAE SALVATIONIS

A hundred years or so after the *BP* was complied, in the first part of the fourteenth century a similar typological guidebook appeared. The *Speculum Humanae Salvationis* (henceforth: *SHS*) was, like the *BP*, a visual and verbal compendium, but larger in scope and design. Like the *BP* again, this immense handbook (very much in the line of contemporary theological *summas*) could serve as a source-book for preachers. The *SHS* must have been a best-seller in its time, because three hundred and ninety-four manuscripts have survived. It was written in Latin but presumably due to its enormous popularity it was soon translated into German, English, Dutch, French and Czech as well. Like the *BP*, the *SHS* was also among the earliest printed books. It was printed from moveable types and its woodcuts were influenced by the blockbook edition of the *BP*.[58] In their richly illustrated and documented edition, the American book-historians Adrian Wilson and Joyce Lancester Wilson have convincingly demonstrated that the *SHS* occupied a unique place in the history of the book. 'It is the only medieval work that exists in manuscripts, in blockbooks, and in sixteen later incunabula.'[59]

About the author of the compendium we know practically nothing. From the book Emile Mâle concludes that 'the author was a man who lived in the last part of the thirteenth century and was permeated by its spirit'[60] but most recent scholarship suggests that the *SHS* was compiled probably between 1310–1324.[61] A short note attributed to the author appears on some manuscripts: 'the book called *Speculum Humanae Salvationis* is a new compilation, edited by an author who, out of humility, wanted to conceal his name.'[62]

But the anonymous author, for all his humility, seems to have been ambitious to outdo his predecessor in the scale of his project. First of all, he places his typological programme into a large verbal context, a long rhymed prose. Secondly, he invariably gives three prefigurations for each New Testament event. The New Testament scene, the antitype usually comes first and is followed by three types from the Old Testament. A superficial comparison of these two visual compendia reveals that the richer and more ambitious programme of the *SHS* is, however, much less biblical than the *BP*. It is not, we contend, because, in Mâle's words 'the author often found himself in trouble . . . as it was not easy to find three passages in the Old Testament',[63] but because his intention was much more mariological than christological. In the author's theology the Virgin Mary appears as a co-redemptor. Her story precedes and follows Christ's story, though in most cases it is analogous to it. Mary's maternal function provides a framework for Christ's ministry and redemptive death. Her role, *before* and *after* this ministry of Christ, is seen to *complete* her Son's redemption. As this is not a biblical idea, the author, in his choice of the antitypes and especially of the types, had to turn to extrabiblical sources in most cases. The images of the annunciation and the nativity of Christ are preceded by the nativity and even the annunciation of the Virgin. The images devoted to the Virgin are again numerous at the end of the cycle, after the events of Pentecost. The author's most important extrabiblical sources were the *Historia Scholastica* of Petrus Comestor (died in 1179), the *Legenda Aurea* written in the 1260s by Jacobus de Voragine and the *Summa Theologica* of St Thomas Aquinas.[64]

The text in the *SHS*, as we have suggested, carries for much more weight than in the *BP*. Each group, consisting of four images, is followed by a long commentary in rhymed prose. The text merits attention on its own account and there are even unillustrated manuscripts of the *SHS*.

The Structure

For our discussion of the *SHS* it seems advisable once again to refer to a single edition, which in this case will be a Middle English translation of the *SHS* entitled *The Mirour of Mans Saluacioune* and edited by Avril Henry.[65] Occasionally we shall refer to a fine edition of the woodcuts by Wilson and Wilson but our reading will, in large part, be guided by the scholarly and critical insights of Avril Henry.

The structure of the *SHS* can be divided as follows:

1. *Prologus*: 100 lines, explaining the author's aim
2. *Prohemium* or the Table of Chapters
3. *Chapters* 1–42.

The main body of the work. Each chapter, consisting of 100 lines, is composed of four events and four illustrations. Chapters 3–42 are typological. The story of Christ is embedded into the story of Mary.

4. *Chapters* 43–45.

There is an interesting remark in the compendium concerning the practical use of the book as it was intended by the author. He suggests that preachers who are unable to buy the whole book could purchase simply the summary of the chapter-contents (*Prohemium*) which they could conveniently use in their sermons. Even if they were unfamiliar with the stories they could use it as an *aid-memoire*.

Emile Mâle has demonstrated that manuscripts of the *SHS* were widely available in the Low countries. He even provides evidence that artists like Jan Van Eyck or Roger van der Weyden possessed a manuscript copies of it in their studios.[66] Perhaps the best known artistic application of the *SHS* is by Dirck Bouts (c.1415–1475) who was commissioned to paint an altarpiece devoted to the Eucharist for the church of St. Pierre in Louvain and this he painted on the basis of Chapter XVI of the *SHS*.[67]

The Reading of a Group. An Example (Chapter XXIII)

In selecting a particular chapter of the *SHS* for attention I hope to be able to illustrate again how the material lends itself to the composition of a sermon.

The four pictures of Chapter XXIII are as follows:

1) Christ prays for his torturers
2) Tubalcain's forge: the discovery of music

3) The martyrdom of Isaias
4) Moab sacrifices his son

Each scene is described in a long Prologue. We read about chapter XXIII as follows:

> The XXIII chapitle seith [h]ow Crist was nailed on Rode tree
> And prayed for his crucyfiours of his ineffable pitiee.
> Jubal, fynder of musik, figured this thing properelye,
> Finding in Tubalkaym hamers the tunes of melodye.
> So Crist, as he was ruthfully hamerd apon the Croce,
> Songe to his Fadire of heven in full swete voice:
> So swete and faire was it, and full of all dulcoure,
> Tat it convertid thre thovzand men in tat ilk one houre,
> And Ysay this crucifixioune also prefigured.
> Wham Manasses with a sawe of tree slew and departid.
> It was prefigured by King [Moab] when he would sacrifice
>   his son to the Lord
> So that God should release his city from the siege.

The New Testament scene is the nailing of Christ to the cross. The previous chapter had described and illustrated how he carried the cross. Isaac obediently carrying the wood was seen, as usual, to be the prefiguration of Christ obediently carrying his cross. In chapter XXIII Christ's hands and feet are just being nailed to the cross. Amongst the three prefigurations the martyrdom of Isaias is extrabiblical: the legendary account taken from Petrus Comestor. The text suggests that the division of Isaias' body into two by the saw is a prefiguration of the separation of Jesus' soul from his body. The third type is also unusual: it illustrates the story of the Gentile King Moab, sacrificing his own son on the walls of the city in order to save his people from famine (2 King 3:27).

Perhaps, most intriguing and chilling of all in this context is the reference to the Sons of Lamech. It is recorded in Genesis 4 that the son of Lamech's first wife was called Jubal 'the father of all such as handle the harp and organ' (4:21). The son of Lamech's second wife was named Tubalcain and we learn that he was 'an instructor of every artificer in brass and iron' (4:22). Traditionally they have been seen as the inventors of melody and smithery. The *SHS* states, that while Tubalcain the smith was making sound resonate by hammering on an anvil in his forge, Jubal the musician was making a melody out of this sound, and the picture also depicts them as they are at work around the anvil. This surprizing association of the two craftsmanships becomes extraordinarily significant when the simultaneous process of sound-making and melody-composing is seen as a prefiguration of Christ praying for his enemies whilst his hands and feet are being nailed to the cross. The implications astonish and perhaps appall the reader. Just as music is forged from the violent hammering on an anvil, Jesus' prayer for his executioners: 'Father forgive them for they know not what they do' (Luke 23:34) is wrung from him as the nails are hammered violently through his body.

The text says:

For when the crucifiours hamered Crist to the Crosse wodely,
That Lord for thaim to his Fadere sange fulle swete melodye:
'Fadere, forgif to thaym, for thai ne wote what thai do,
Thai ne knawe me noght for thi Son that thay do thus unto.'

According to the analogical logic of typology apparently unconnected, far-fetched texts can be superimposed on one another. Within this one 'intertext' alone, there is considerable drama, music and poetry.

A Comparison: The 'Intertexts' of the CRUCIFIXION in the Klosterneuburg Altar (KA), the Biblia Pauperum (BP) and the Speculum Humanae Salvationis (SHS)

KA: Isaac Offered Crucifixion   BP: Isaac Offered Crucifixion
    Two Spies and the Grape   Brazen Serpent
SHS: Crucifixion Nebuchadnezzar's Dream about the Tree
     King Codrus Sacrifices Himself for the People
     Eleazar Stabbing an Elephant and Crushed by It

We have seen that in the *KA* the crucifixion constituted the symmetrical centre of the whole composition. The offering of Isaac is an extremely conventional prefiguration of God's sacrifice of his son. The image of the two spies carrying the bunch of grapes on a wooden pole suggests at first only a formal resemblance (Christ's body hanging over the cross the bunch of grape hanging over the wooden pole). However, the symbolism is perhaps more sacramental than formal: one can associate the grapes (or wine as the product of grapes) with the blood of Christ. (We may note in passing that in the *BP* the two spies returning from the Promised Land are seen as the prefiguration of baptism rather than crucifixion. This correspondence seems surprizing initially. The exposition is given in the *lectio*, namely, that on their way back to bring home the grapes, these spies cross the river Jordan. Though this crossing is different from the crossing of the Red Sea, nevertheless the *BP*, as Henry suggests, 'brilliantly conflates two events to stress the bloodshed implicit in the Baptism'.[68] According to Roman 6: 3–4 in baptism one is baptised 'into' the death of Christ.) Finally, in the *SHS* the two spies are seen as the prefiguration of Christ carrying the cross. In summary then, the two spies foreshadow the crucifixion in the *KA*, the baptism in the *BP*, and Christ carrying the cross in the *SHS*. The *BP* adopts the commoner and more conventional type of the Brazen serpent as a prefiguration of the crucifixion.

In the *SHS* the crucifixion is first prefigured by the story of Nebuchadnezzar's dream about the tree (Daniel 4: 7–28). The text of the *SHS* explains that the huge tree which is to be cut down in Nebuchadnezzar's dream is a foreshadowing of the Messiah. The roots that are to be preserved, prefigure the disciples who are left to carry on even if their master is fallen. The second type is the extrabiblical story of King Codrus borrowed from Valerianus Maximus.[69] According to the story, King Codrus is killed at his own request for the sake of his people. In most versions he is depicted as clothed in a servant's attire which again prefigures the sacrifice of Jesus who also dresses himself in human flesh in order to deliver human kind from its enemies. The last type is perhaps the most original. The story of Eleazar is taken from the apocryphal (deuterocanonical) book of Maccabees (1 Maccabbees 6:42–6). The scene depicts Eleazar beneath an elephant mounted by his enemies. Heroically, Eleazar runs his sword into the elephant from below. The elephant collapses and dies thereby crushing Eleazar himself. By this action Eleazar prefigures Christ who also sacrifices his own life to save his people.

THE IMPACT OF THE TYPOLOGICAL VISION ON MEDIAEVAL ART

It seems to us that the application of typology in the twelfth and the thirteenth centuries was perhaps simpler than in the fourteenth or fifteenth centuries but from a biblical point of view, it was much purer and perhaps more intact than in the centuries that followed. This is illustrated by the way how the author of the *SHS* 'rewrote' the *BP*. The *SHS* preserved the central typological idea of prefiguration and fulfilment in its juxtaposing of images, but by trying to extend the scope of the work or to enrich the material, the *SHS* frequently lost the illuminating power, the expressive energy and the rhetorical simplicity of its predecessor. In some of the individual groups, nevertheless, many original analogies and insights were developed.

The wide-spread popularity of these visual and verbal compendia as 'typological dictionaries' can be demonstrated by reference to medieval paintings, cathedral-windows and tapestries. We have for example, already alluded to Dirck Bouts' painting of the Eucharist in St. Peter's Church, Louvain. Emile Mâle, in his *Religious Art in France*, still a classic in its field, discusses the typological portal of the cathedral of Vienne (France) and mentions the typological frescoes in the cathedral of Brixen (Tirol).[70] Of course, it is not my intention to suggest that *all* typological art in the Middle Ages was influenced by the compendia I have just discussed, but their influence on the art of cathedral-windows is still to be investigated, and in fact, a study of the 'sermons' of these 'speaking' typological cathedral-windows could be the subject-matter of an entire monograph. At this point, however, we have to be satisfied with reference simply to some of the most well-known examples. Emile Mâle has surveyed the most famous examples of the stained glasses in the French cathedrals of Bourges, Chartres, La Mans, Tours, Lyons and Rouen.[71] The windows of Chartres cathedral particularly, have been given considerable scholarly attention.[72] To give an example of German typological cathedral-windows we may refer to the stained glasses of a side chapel in Cologne-cathedral.[73] And in England,[74] we have already alluded to the windows of Canterbury cathedral.[75] Of typological stained-glass panels in the 15th century church of Tattershall, Lincolnshire six are now at St Martin's of Stamford, four in Burghley House, Nottinghamshire and some fragments have been reset in the chapel at Warwick Castle.[76] There is also a typological glass-panel in the Lady Chapel in Exeter cathedral.[77] Perhaps the most famous English example is, the Flemish-designed typological stained glass in King's College Chapel, Cambridge.[78] A less well-known example can be found in the church of Fairford, Gloucester.

Finally, mention must be made about what is probably the most beautiful 'rewriting' of the *BP*. This 'rewriting' – in fact, a tapestry – is part of a collection of tapestries now to be found in the abbey of Chaise Dieu (Haute-Loire).[79] These originally Flemish tapestries contain even the texts of the *BP* and in most cases they are almost exact copies. With its vivid and harmonious colours this tapestry has indeed converted the 'poverty' and noble simplicity of the *BP* into a 'rich', impressive work of art.

5
Reading Literature

FROM PREFIGURATION TO POSTFIGURATION

> Omnis mundi creatura
> quasi liber et pictura
> nobis est et speculum:
> nostrae vitae, nostrae mortis,
> nostri status, nostrae sortis
> fidele signaculum.[1]

This short poem from Alan of Lille from the twelfth century illustrates very well the figurative view of reality characteristic of the medieval period. In Chapter 4 we looked at the principle of 'pictura quasi scriptura' which implies that 'picture' can be conceived of as a figuration and thus a fulfilment or completion, of 'Scripture'. By exploring this principle we hoped to gain some sort of biblical justification for the visual arts in opposition to such extreme iconoclastic views inherent in the antivisual prejudice. This short poem takes us a step further, inviting us to extend the idea of biblical figuration. Alan's song perceives the whole created world 'quasi liber et pictura'. This involves the notion that the whole world – including nature and history, as well as the human individual – constitutes God's grand design. Each item of the created world is a sign pointing to the Creator: in semiotic terms, God is the 'signifier' and the world the 'signified'. Gabriel Josipovici in a seminal essay on 'The World as a Book' quotes Hugh of St Victor:

> For this whole world is a book written by the finger of God, that is, created by divine power; and individual creatures are as figures therein not devised by human will but instituted by divine authority to show forth the invisible things of God.[2]

As in the visual arts, so in literature, the typological mode of biblical thought has left its mark. And literature does not simply imitate or illustrate typology but adopts this biblical mode of thought and develops it further. The essays in Earl Miner's *Literary Uses of Typology from the Middle Ages to the Present* (1977)[3] provide an excellent introduction to this subject. In view of the literary adaptation of typology, however, the traditional conception of typology as 'prefiguration' is clearly insufficient. In secular literature, biblical typology is 'displaced' (Northrop Frye's term), and literary figures can be seen as 'subfulfilling' (A. C. Charity's term) biblical figures. As with the individual (cf. Milton's notion that the ultimate authority is the human heart), literature can be seen as a fulfilment or completion of Scripture in so far as literature makes a further sense of Scripture. What I have in mind is not an allegorical commentary on Scripture (this idea would turn literature into an 'ornament', or the beautiful illustration of the 'high truth of Scripture'). Instead of such dualistic, Platonic views I am suggesting the notion of creative application, the idea of literary recreation. Literary recreation can, in fact, be called *postfiguration*. Murray Roston, in his book on *Biblical Drama in England*, suggests that postfiguration as a 'complete reversal of prefiguration' appeared at the end of the Middle Ages when the haloed biblical saints were replaced by realistic characters of flesh and blood on the medieval stage. Thus Noah was much more a 'master craftsman of the local shipbuilders' guild' than an Old Testament Jew. Roston argues that postfiguration became more decisive and characteristic for Protestants because of their growing concern with the Covenant tradition:

> For if the covenant reaffirmed throughout the generations was contracted with the individual as well as the group, then the Protestant's *own life* should bear the marks of that cyclical repetition. As he read the biblical tales of the patriarchs, prophets, and kings . . . the Protestant looked for their true meaning in his own spiritual and even political exertions. He began to see himself in biblical terms, re-enacting or 'postfiguring' in his life leading incidents from the lives of the scriptural heroes . . . The Puritans sailing towards the New World proclaimed that they were bound for the Promised Land . . . their voyage was for them a seventeenth-century cyclical re-enactment of the Exodus from Egypt. Milton, the discarded champion of God longing for revenge on his enemies, instinctively saw himself a reworking of Samson eyeless in Gaza. And implicit in this postfiguration

was the encouraging conviction that the victorious destiny of the biblical hero was, by virtue of the other parallels, the destiny of the postfigurer too; so that Milton in his spiritual darkness found some comfort in the belief that his salvation must lie before him.[4]

Roston adds that in the Catholic Middle Ages 'such intensely personal identification with scriptural heroes would have been regarded as presumptuous and was relegated to generalized homiletical parallels encouraging the Christian to emulate the virtues and shun the vices of a Noah or Esau, it now became the inspiration of the militant Protestant as he brandished his sword or pen with the fervour of his spiritual forebears'.[5]

Roston's insights are persuasive but I think we should not regard this attitude as a mere sectarian extravagance on the part of Milton and other Protestants. There was nothing extraordinary or perverse in what they were doing. They were conscientious readers of the Bible and they simply obeyed what the Bible demanded from them: completion, fulfilment, identification; they were simply 'filling up the measures' of their 'fathers', the biblical figures. We have seen in Chapter 3 that this was how Jesus and the first Christians read Scripture. Behind the Protestant emphasis of the *analogia fidei* ('analogy of faith') against the Catholic *analogia entis* ('analogy of being'), there is, undoubtedly, an 'analogy of interpretation' or an 'analogy of reading'. In their 're-enactment' of the lives of the Old Testament figures, they were employing an interpretative mechanism, or reading, inherent in Scripture. They did not arbitrarily or illegitimately identify themselves with these figures, but having appropriated Scripture, they felt thath they were absorbed, or swallowed up by the 'Book' and, thus, rightly considered themselves to be part of that book.

In the following pages I shall present some 'case-studies', or readings, of particular works of literature. Each of them will be a drama, selected from different periods of literary history. My first case-study is a 'text-book example': a play from an English medieval mystery-cycle. The two other plays chosen may seem somewhat surprising at first sight, as they have not been subjected previously to explicitly typological analysis. My second case study, then, will concentrate on possible figurative readings of Shakespeare's *Measure for Measure*. And thirdly, I shall attempt to construct a figurative interpretation of T. S. Eliot's *Murder in the Cathedral*. My aim in selecting these plays, is to prove that possibilities in figurative reading or interpretation point far beyond the rigid, traditional view of typology. Let us recall what Auerbach said about figurative interpretation:

> Figural interpretation establishes a connection between two events or persons, the first of which signifies not only itself but also the second, while the second encompasses or fulfills the first.[6]

Here Auerbach is, of course, concerned with biblical typology *par excellence* which is to be seen and understood in an historical context. Therefore the 'events' or 'persons' are meant to be 'real' historical events, which, as we have seen earlier, carry a surplus of meaning. However, we can translate Auerbach's idea of 'historical' reality into 'textual' (including fictitious) reality. Again applying Kristeva's term of 'intertextuality', I propose to modify Auerbach's definition as follows:

> Figural interpretation establishes a connection between two *textual* events or persons, the first of which signifies not only itself but also the second, while the second encompasses or fulfills the first.

In terms of literature 'fiction' (a play or a character) may stand for what Auerbach understood as 'historical' reality. All the three plays work in terms of intertextuality: each of them can be seen as a text on a biblical 'architext' (G. Genette's term) whether it is the Genesis, the Sermon on the Mount in the Gospel, or St Stephen's speech in the Acts of the Apostles. We can call the biblical text an 'architext', and the literary text a 'supertext'. In figural interpretation both architext and supertext are 'real' – that is, neither of them is a pretext for the other. It is this that distinguishes figural from allegorical interpretation. In other words, if the supertext is only a pretext for the architext we have to do with allegory. However, it is more frequently the case in modern literature, that the architext is a pretext for the supertext, and thus there is no necessary relationship between their 'realities', or, to put it another way, the architext in this case is not 'real', it cannot retain its own integrity and validity within the new context. In figural interpretation, however, both the architext and the supertext are *real* and *valid*. The supertext as postfiguration is a fulfilment or recreation of the architext. We have to emphasize this fictional reality or integrity because otherwise these plays could easily be charged with being mere allegories or 'illustrations' of the biblical texts. But as fulfilment is 'real', these plays are also to be seen as 'real' plays and they are to be read or seen *as plays* and not as didactic demonstrations of certain biblical passages or doctrines. Postfiguration means that these plays carry a surplus of meaning which they gain from the architext. Just as an Old Testament hero like Moses was 'real' whilst also carrying a surplus of meaning as the prefiguration or type of Christ, the plays are also 'real' plays whilst simultaneously postfiguring some aspects of the architext. We have said that allegory is alien from postfiguration because it illustrates concepts. However, postfiguration seems to show close kinship with the genre of the parable, which is exemplification.

Auerbach has grasped the significance of the reality-principle in the figural interpretation of medieval literature:

> It is precisely the figural interpretation of reality which, though in constant conflict with purely spiritualist or Neoplatonic tendencies, was the dominant view in European Middle Ages: the idea that earthly life is thoroughly real, with the reality of the flesh into which the logos entered, but with all its reality it is only *umbra* and *figura* of the authentic, future, ultimate truth, the real reality that will unveil and preserve the *figura*. In this way the individual earthly event . . . is viewed primarily in immediate vertical connection with a divine order which encompasses it.[7]

What Auerbach said of prefiguration seems to be valid of postfiguration as well. In postfiguration an architext is recreated by a supertext, each of them being real, valid and dynamic. The postfiguring supertext gains its power and energy from the architext and therefore, the supertext is 'transparent'. Supertexts that use architexts only as pretexts are opaque.

In all the three plays we are going to study the dynamics of this intertextuality, whether these supertexts can be seen as transparent postfigurations, fulfilments, or parables, of the biblical architexts.

DRAMATIC HERMENEUTICS IN THE 'ABRAHAM AND ISAAC' PLAY OF THE CHESTER CYCLE (PAGINA IV)

We have suggested that the literary adaptation of typology is essentially postfiguration rather than prefiguration. However, literature, especially at an earlier, naive stage, has been concerned with the imitation, or the 'acting out' of prefiguration. The Fathers read the Old Testament in a prefigurative way and their readings were undoubtedly echoed in sermons. We have also seen that prefiguration was absorbed by medieval art and this art whether in the *Biblia Pauperum*, or the *Speculum Humanae Salvationis*, or in the lay-out of cathedral windows, was meant to delight and educate the Christian in God's grand design. God, the designer, was frequently conceived of as an artist and his art was the grand design of salvation-history. As early as the second century, in a beautiful poem *On Pascha*, Melito of Sardis praised God as an artist who is able to envisage the future reality in his 'model' or 'prefiguration'. (The original Greek uses the words *typos* and *parabole*).[8] The same idea was taken up by John Chrysostom in the fourth century. Typology and salvation history were understood as the characteristics of God's art.

It is clear that art and literature were inspired by what was understood as the art of God. From the fourteenth century the typological symbolism of the cathedral windows was acted out each year on Corpus Christi Day in the open air, in the moving pageants of enthusiastic guildsmen. Sincere piety and religious laughter went hand in hand and medieval man felt himself at home in God's grand cosmic and comic universe. The spectators, the men and women in the street, were offered a view of the panorama of God's salvation history: the time spanned from Creation to Doomsday within the cycle of a single day. Eternity was experienced in time and time in eternity. Moreover, the audience was able to participtate, becoming a part of what was happening in the pageants. Thus the audience was part of the mob at the crucifixion, but could also feel itself to be witness to the resurrection. The minds of medieval men and women were well-trained in typology. For them there was nothing extraordinary in seeing the role of Abel taken by the same person who was playing Christ. But even if they had not already been aware that Noah's ark was the type of the church in which men and women are saved if they enter by baptism, or that the flood is the prefiguration of the final judgement, they could have gained some insights from the words and the gestures of the players.

We may wonder how the individual episodes were typologically structured within the same cycle. V. A. Kolve in his pioneering book *The Play Called Corpus Christi* (1966)[9] provided a useful diagram to show the complex formal organization of the Corpus

Christi cycle, how figures and their fulfilments are theologically related to one-another:

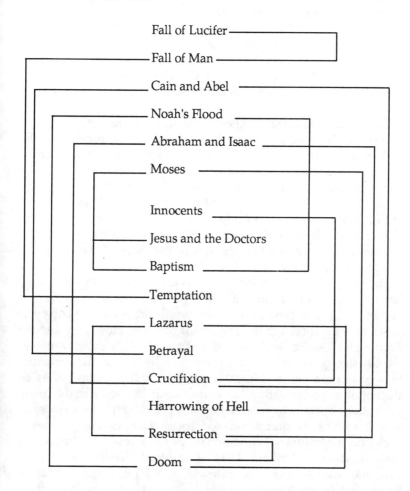

The Old Testament episode that was most frequently read in a prefigurative way, was the story of Abraham and Isaac. In the arrangement of the *KA* and of the *BP* we have seen how often the story of Abraham, including his encounter with Melchizedek and the sacrifice of Isaac, was presented as a type. The Abraham-cycle was perhaps the most significant source of inspiration for prefigurative reading. There has been a strong patristic tradition from Tertullian onwards including Origen, St Ambrose and

St Augustine, that Abraham's sacrifice of his own son was a type of the crucifixion. St Thomas Aquinas is said to have composed the office for the feast of Corpus Christi:

> In figuris praesignatur
> cum Isaac immolatur,
> agnus Paschae deputatur,
> datur manna patribus.[10]

Whilst in the Genesis story Abraham is the main character and Isaac is very much in the background, in the typological exegesis of the Fathers the focus was shifted from Abraham to Isaac, whose innocence and obedience were seen to have prefigured the innocence and obedience of Christ, probably on the basis of Romans 5:19 and Philippians 2:8. This was reflected not only in the KA or in the BP but in hundreds of other examples of visual art. In the windows of Canterbury cathedral, for example, the wood carried by Isaac for the sacrifice, is arranged on his back in the shape of the cross. The image's typological rhetoric is evident.

The story of Abraham and Isaac has also survived in seven English medieval plays, including one in Cornish.[11] Apart from the four cycle-plays, the Abraham and Isaac episode occurs in two non-cycle plays as well: these are the Dublin (or Northampton) play and the Brome-play. As we shall attempt to show, of all the seven versions, the Chester-cycle has probably preserved the best dramatic balance between figure and fulfilment. Naturally, each version builds on the notion of prefiguration, but in the Ludus Conventriae (N-Town) cycle, Isaac appears to be too righteous, pleading for his own death, and this gives the drama a melodramatic flavour. The Towneley-cycle, on the contrary, overemphasizes the human weaknesses of both Isaac and Abraham. Here Isaac pleads hysterically for his own life and Abraham, a spineless, timid man, is so afraid of Sarah that he contemplates lying to her. In the York cycle there is much dramatic tension, but Isaac, being thirty, is perhaps too overtly the prefiguration of Christ. He is not only pious but wise, he is almost setting an example for his father. However, at the end, the tragedy of near-sacrifice is converted almost to a comedy as, the climax being over, Abraham is tries to persuade Isaac to get married soon. The non-cycle Dublin (Northampton) version is perhaps the most true to life. Sarah appears at the beginning and at the end of the episode and Isaac constantly refers to the sorrow of his mother before the abortive sacrifice. Sarah's characterization of the shrewish wife is convincing. When Abraham tells her that he is to sacrifice their son, Sarah's natural abhorrence: 'Would you have slain my son Isaac? . . . where was your mind?' is in excellent counterpoint to the saintliness of Abraham who replies: 'My mind? – upon the good Lord on high!'[12]

It is the non-cycle Brome play that comes nearest to the Chester-play, and scholars have, in fact, argued, that it may have influenced the Chester-version. Isaac's obedience, innocence and nobility serve to increase the dramatic tension, and his words before the sacrifice are the very words of the agonized Christ on the cross:

> Ah! Father of heaven, to thee I cry, Lord, receive me into thy hand.[13]

David Bevington rightly praises the play as follows: 'The account is remarkable for its ballad-like simplicity, its intense portrayal of filial and parental tenderness, and its sustaining of dramatic tension. The effect is touching and, although daringly close to pathos, never guilty of mawkishness.'[14]

Pagina IV of the Chester cycle is an attempt to condense three episodes of the Abraham-cycle into one single play. The play begins with the Melchizedek episode. Abraham and Lot, having returned from their victory over four kings offer their 'teath' (tithe) through God's priest, Melchizedek. Melchizedek offers them bread and wine. After the short episode, the 'Expositor' appears on the stage. The Expositor figure appears only in the Chester-cycle and there only in five of the twenty-four plays. It is in the Abraham-play in which he appears for the first time. His task is to explain the typological significance of the scene. He has to show that this scene foreshadows the Eucharist:

> This present, I saye veramente,
> signifieth the newe testamente
> that nowe is used with good intente
> throughout all Christianitye.
>
> In the owld lawe, without leasinge,
> when these two good men were livinge,
> of beastes were there offeringe
> and eke there sacramente.

> But synce Christe dyed one roode-tree,
> in bred and wyne his death remember wee;
> and his last supper our mandee
> was his commandemente. (ll. 17–28)[15]

When the scene is over the dialogue is continued between God and Abraham, and this on-going dialogue provides continuity between the episodes. The second episode is very brief: God promises descendants ('seed') to Abraham and orders the institution of circumcision, that 'eache man-chylde one the eyght daye bee circumsysed'. This is going to be the sign by which God recognizes the people who belong to him. From God's part it is a sign of covenant, from man's part it is an act of obedience. The Expositor appears on stage again and explains to the spectators that the circumcision is a prefiguration of baptism and that God's promise to Abraham that among his multiple descendants 'one chylde of greate degree all mankynde shall forbye' is clearly a reference to Christ's redemption.

Finally after these two preliminary episodes, we get to the story of Abraham and Isaac. When God summons Abraham to sacrifice his son, Abraham's reaction is an act of immediate obedience. Straight away, he is ready to fulfill God's commandment. He asks Isaac to prepare for the journey, telling him that 'for we must doe a little thinge'. The dramatist emphasizes that Isaac obeys his father as Abraham obeys his heavenly Father: this is the analogy or typology of obedience. The tenderness, the gentleness and magnanimity of Isaac are hard for Abraham to bear: 'my harte will breake in three!' Isaac's integrity of character serves only to enhance the Father's anguish. The dialogue between Abraham and Isaac grows in dramatic intensity. Isaac becomes more and more disturbed by his father's 'heavye chere' and the lack of any beast to be sacrificed, and he is understandably alarmed when he sees that his father has drawn out his sword. When Abraham at last reveals: 'I muste thee kyll', Isaac pleads for his own life, appealing with natural, human emotion to his father to spare him on account of his childish innocence, especially for the sake of his mother who would kneel to plead for the life of her son. Critics have suggested that the reader, or the spectator, is expected to conflate Sarah's sorrow with the sorrow of the Virgin. However, once Isaac has understood that his sacrifice is God's commandment, he stops pleading for his own life and is immediately willing to obey. He falls upon his knees and asks the blessings and the forgiveness of his father. But Isaac does not become an abstract, inhuman figure even in this act of perfect obedience: he asks his father to do the act quickly, and to provide him with a handkerchief so that he should not see the sword. He even encourages his father, now deploring what he has to do, to carry out the deed without delay: 'A, mercye, father, why tarrye yee soe? Smite of my head and lett mee goe.' His farewell and the way he remembers his mother and brothers immediately evokes the image of Christ who from the cross bids his favourite disciple to take care of his mother. Isaac's 'last' words again echo Christ's words from the cross:

> Almighty God in majestie,
> my soule I offer unto thee.
> Lorde, to yt bee kynde.   (ll. 418–20)

At the crucial moment angels appear to withhold Abraham's sword and they point to the 'horned wether' among the briars as a substitute victim for Isaac. At the end God also appears to praise Abraham for his obedience. His words are straightforward echoes of Romans 8:32: 'He hath spared not his own Son, but delivered him up for us all'. Thus says the Lord of the play:

> Abraham, by my selfe I sweare:
> for thou hast bine obedient ayere,
> and spared not thy sonne to teare
> to fulfill my byddinge,'   (ll. 444–6)

The Expositor appears for the third time to explain 'this significatyon':

> By Abraham I may understand
> the Father of heaven that cann fonde
> with his Sonnes blood to breake that bonde
> that the dyvell had brought us to.
> By Isaack understande I maye
> Jesus that was obedyent aye,
> his Fathers will to worke alwaye
> and death for confounde.'   (ll. 468–75)

A modern critical impulse might suggest that the arbitrary imposition of this figure on the dramatic structure kills the play and makes a didactic sermon out of it. But we should not forget that in the Middle Ages art was not strictly divorced from teaching: teaching was art and art was teaching. We have noticed this healthy balance between art and didacticism in the *BP*. Peter W. Travis is surely right to suggest that 'Figural correspondences are revealed most easily in stasis, as in the graphic arts, or in biblical commentary. In drama, the form best suited to typological demonstration is normally an emblematic vignette (as here), or a tableau vivant momentarily frozen within the ongoing mimetic action.'[16] But Travis' reservation that typology places 'restraints' upon the drama is less convincing. Emblematic structures in drama, as recent critics have argued, may indeed help to deepen our appreciation of these scenes without destroying their dramatic structure. Probably much depends on how the play is directed: if the emblematic scenes are played too directly or in too overt a manner, they may be unconvincing, but gestures or even momentarily frozen scenes may provoke associations that enrich the performance of the play.

'LIKE POWER DIVINE' – FIGURATION AND META-DRAMA SHAKESPEARE'S *MEASURE FOR MEASURE*

The example I have chosen for my next case-study is far from being a conventional piece of typological symbolism like some of the poems by Donne, Herbert or Milton. I certainly do not wish to claim that my reading of the play is going to lay bare a previously hidden typological structure within the drama. Instead, I wish to play with the possibility of various figurative readings of this comedy. Shakespeare's *Measure for Measure* is usually regarded as a 'dark comedy' or a 'problem play'. The reason why critics consider three comedies of Shakespeare as distinct from the romantic comedies is that these comedies are claimed to be more 'realistic', lacking the elements of the supernatural or magic. However, this separation is arbitrary, because here a comic magic is also at work, even if translated to more prosaic terms: in two of the 'problem-plays' as Northrop Frye observed, 'the chief magical device used is the bed-trick instead of enchanted forests or identical twins.'[17]

Nevertheless *Measure for Measure* is one of the most enigmatic plays of Shakespeare. Interpretations of the drama have diverged radically from one another. The reaction of critics has ranged from high praise and enthusiasm to contempt and disgust. In teaching the play at university I have experienced at first hand how emotionally explosive an issue, for example, is evaluation of Isabella's character. Student opinion for and against Isabella clashed violently, the majority severely condemning her rigid hypocrisy while a minority tried to defend her. The Duke's character has likewise been the subject-matter of hot debate: he has been read both as an unmotivated madman and as the incarnation in Vienna of Divine Providence.

To what are these controversial and diametrically opposed reactions due? They are probably due to the fact that the characters and the issues raised are complex, and moreover that the play itself is extremely puzzling and enigmatic, demanding or even provoking interpretation! Indeed, one cannot but feel that this drama is *about* interpretation. For what is interpretation? As Ricoeur said it is the deciphering of symbols and symbols are twofold linguistic expressions that demand interpretation. A symbol simultaneously covers and manifests, hides and proclaims, conceals and reveals. A symbol, as a Hungarian writer once put it, 'conceals what it reveals and reveals what it conceals'.[18] Does this mean that we conceive Shakespeare's *Measure for Measure* as a 'symbol'?

It has been suggested above that a figurative interpretation does not annul the 'reality' of the play as a play but it recognizes that the play carries a surplus of meaning and that this interpretation tries to read the play in terms of this surplus. If our reading conceives of the drama as a symbol it means that we have recognized that the structure of the play is very much reminiscent of our definition of a symbol. Why? Because the play itself is also structured on the principles of hiding and uncovering, concealment and revelation, closure and disclosure. The structure of this play is similar to the structure of a symbol in so far as Duke Vincentio conceals himself in disguise not only to learn about his people, nor to test them, but because he also wants to teach them: he does not merely wish to 'know' but he wishes to 'let them know'. What he cannot achieve directly and manifestly, he will be able to accomplish by concealment and deception, in secrecy and disguise. Only by hiding himself as a *deus absconditus* can he uncover the vices of Vienna, only by concealing his identity can he reveal the truth about the real impulses of the human heart. The last scene is a successive revelation in the course of which he is gradually liberating the oppressed truth from the chains of a pseudo-reality. The Duke is indeed the deputy dramatist, if not the dramatist himself. The Duke as plot-achitect or director wishes to hold truth up as a mirror to human nature so that after the repentance of his puppet-figures he can practise his merciful generosity. Shakespeare's play is at the same time the Duke's grand 'game' which he is to win although from time to time he might find himself on the verge of losing it. His name (Vincentio) is an adumbration of that victory which he is meant to manifest.

Before developing our own view of the play as a meta-drama or meta-comedy with the Duke being both architect and interpreter of the plot (in fact, a distant descendent of the Expositor-figure of the miracle play), we are going to take a brief look at three figurative interpretations of the play. These interpretations are stimulating, though perhaps, in some cases, controversial.

The first significant figurative interpretation appears in an essay of G. Wilson Knight: *'Measure for Measure* and the Gospels'.[19] As his title indicates, Knight's essay offers an intertextual reading of the play. Knight's thesis implies the notion that the architext is not necessarily the 'source' of the play (Whetstone's *Promos and Cassandra*) but a text that determines the tone and the colouring of the supertext. For Knight what we mean by architext is undoubtedly the Gospel. He substantiates his thesis by discussing the comedy's title which is taken from the Sermon on the Mount (Matthew 7:1). Naturally, since the play's central theme is that of law and mercy, the reader is immediately put in mind of the association between the Old and the New Testaments. (The thematic resonance is the same in *The Merchant of Venice*.) Knight's reading of the text of the play as parallel to the texts of Scripture is impressive, if occasionally overdone. He finds that 'there is no more beautiful passage in all Shakespeare on the Christian redemption'[20] than Isabella's reply to Angelo when he claims that her brother is a 'forfeit of the law':

> . . . all the souls that were, were forfeit once;
> And He, that might the vantage best have took,
> Found out the remedy. (II, 2, ll. 73–5)

Therefore, says Knight, the central idea of *Measure for Measure* is this: 'And forgive us our debts as we forgive our debtors'.[21] The compelling scriptural resonances throughout the play make for an atmosphere pervaded by Christianity. Knight gives a most intriguing reading of the play set against certain parables in the

Gospels. The parable of the talents, for example, begins as follows: 'For the kingdom of heaven is as a man travelling into a far country, who called his own servants, and delivered unto them his goods' (Matthew 25:14) If the central theme of the play is sin as debt, then the play can be read as an inversion of the parables of The Unmerciful Servant (Matthew 18) or the parable of the Two Debtors (Luke 7). Knight's conclusion is that 'the play must be read not as a picture of normal human affairs, but as a parable, like the parables of Jesus'.[22]

Knight has recognized the 'sublime strangeness' of the parables of Jesus and he has suggested that the strangeness of the play can be understood as sharing this strangeness. If we have Paul Ricoeur's idea of the parable in mind, namely that the parables are meant 'to disorient in order to reorient',[23] we may come even closer to the enigma of the play and the apparent controversial strangeness of the Duke's character. Reorientation by disorientation: this is exactly what the Duke is doing in his plotting of the events. He deceives the people around him (disorientation), but his ultimate purpose is to lead them to a proper self-knowledge and a fresh self-understanding (reorientation). We shall see later that he is, in fact, re-enacting, or plotting the 'divine comedy' and thereby he creates a 'meta-comedy'. At the beginning he 'empties himself' (cf. Philippians 2:6–9) of his office and power, 'takes up the form of a servant', and becomes like one of his men. In mingling with his people and becoming involved in their affairs the Duke can discover what is in their hearts and can work on removing their sins. His descent into the underworld and the prison 'to visit the afflicted spirits' (II, 2, l.4) bears a striking resemblance to Christ's descent into Limbo:'he went and preached unto the spirits in prison' (1 Peter 3:19). And at the beginning of Act V, his theatrical re-appearance accompanied by the sounding of the trumpets immediately evokes in the reader or the spectator the image of the Second Coming, when all that had been hidden becomes manifest and what had been concealed, is revealed. 'Like power divine' (V, 1, l.367) he is indeed come to judge the quick and the dead but he still has to complete his game, he has to unravel the whole situation, showing how his loving mercy is hidden in his judgement. He has to make his people understand that he has played his game for them and not against them, the game was played *for* Angelo, for Isabella, for all the people of Vienna.

We can learn more about the nature of this game if we turn to another figurative reading of the play. In 1946 Roy W. Battenhouse read Shakespeare's *Measure for Measure* as the parable of the Atonement.[24] The story of the Atonement is not explicit in Scripture as a story but it is a doctrine that is 'read out' from Scripture. But despite its being a doctrine it is also a story, or even a 'play', probably the one most central to Christianity. The doctrine is either forgotten by or alien to modern man, including many modern Christians. However, it has been at the core of Christian teaching from the Middle Ages. Perhaps the Reformation marks the shift of interest from the 'objectivity' of redemption to the subjective concern of justification. While the question Anselm of Canterbury asked was: *Cur Deus Homo*? (Why did God become man?), Luther's question concerns his own justification: 'How shall I be saved?' Let us look briefly at the idea of Atonement.[25]

The basic assumption of this doctrine is that God who created the world is good, perfect and holy and therefore that evil is incompatible with his character. But the world is in a state of disorder as men and women have disobeyed their creator. Sin has to be punished and therefore men and women are under the threat of 'decreation', that is, total annihilation. Sin is 'debt' and it is impossible for man to pay what he owes to God for robbing him of his glory. It is impossible for man to make adequate amends. But as God is not merely just but also loving, he does not want the death of his creatures. Only God can achieve what men and women are incapable of doing. He sacrifices his only son who pays the ransom by his obedient death on the cross. It is through Christ's death that the harmony is restored between God and man: therefore his death was an act of atonement ('at-one-ment'), or reconciliation between God and man. Christ's death is a *satisfactio* for God and also a *substitutio* for man. According to the author of the Letter to the Hebrews this expiation of sins was foreshadowed on the Day of Atonement in the Old Testament (Leviticus 23.26ff.).

However, Battenhouse reminds us of another interesting and often forgotten aspect of the Atonement. According to the patristic tradition Satan also has a role in the redemption. A theory about the 'deception of Satan' culminated in Gregory the Great's treatise on the Book of Job. Gregory thought that the redemption of mankind was prefigured in the Book of Job. As human beings are sinful, their 'father', according to Jesus' typological remark in the Gospel of John, is the devil (John 8:44), and in the Book of Job Satan claims that sinful beings are his own property. Thus God has to 'pay' the ransom to Satan too. Therefore he offers his own son as a ransom for mankind to the devil. Christ's cry that he is forsaken by God is the sign that God has indeed passed him on to the devil. Satan is like a great leviathan who devours Christ in his eagerness (the image of the open mouth of the Leviathan is depicted on hundreds of pictures of the Harrowing of the Hell in medieval iconography). Satan is so dazzled by the perfect humanity of Christ that he is happy to accept him as ransom for all those he has swallowed. But in his admiration of Christ's perfect humanity Satan fails to notice his divinity which pierces him through the jaw. Here, then, Christ is the bait and the devil is caught as if on a fisherman's hook. The cross, in fact, has a shape similar to that of a hook, and, moreover, it is frequently depicted as having a real hook at its bottom. For the Church Fathers, God's question to Job: 'Canst thou draw out leviathan with a hook?' (Job 41:1) was a prefiguration of Christ's victory over death. Some claim that the idea of deception may be unworthy of God's character, but some others reply that if Satan, man's enemy, is clever and cunning he can be overcome by somebody who is even more clever and cunning: Christ reminded his disciples to be 'wise as serpents, and harmless as doves' (Matthew 10:16).

But how does this relate to *Measure for Measure*? First of all, this is a play about a series of cunning deceptions. Moreover, words such as 'forfeit', 'ransom', 'remedy', 'redeem', 'redemption', 'satisfaction', 'substitute', or even 'bait' or 'hook' appear quite frequently within the text. For example in Angelo's words when he recognizes his own lust for Isabella:

> O cunning enemy, that to catch a saint,
> With saint dost bait thy hook   (II, 2, ll. 180–1)

And there is a double irony in these words, for not only is Angelo caught thinking of himself as a saint under temptation, but he frames this thought in terms that exactly remind his listeners of how Satan was deceived and caught. Knowing the context we may suspect that Angelo is being presented here as something of a Satan-figure.

Apart from language and imagery the analogy is also compelling on the level of action. If the Duke's 'descent' into the world (and even the underworld) is reminiscent of Christ's entering limbo then there should be a figure that corresponds to Christ's enemy, the

Satan who is meant to be conquered. In this context this might be Angelo. But Angelo is not only Satan (a fallen angel) but also a man. A sinful man, a captive of Satan who is skillfully saved, redeemed and pardoned by the Duke. The Duke's name (Vincentio) evokes the triumphant Christ, the *Christus Victor*. The Duke has to manipulate, manoeuvre and even deceive his 'enemy'. Therefore he plots the *substitutio* of Mariana's body as a *satisfactio* to Angelo. The fact that Angelo does not 'commit fornication' with Isabella but only sleeps with his betrothed wife, just as the fact that the Provost sends him Ragozin's head instead of the head of Claudio, diminishes Angelo's sin. These two subsitutions (because *de facto* he has committed none of these sins) will save his soul. Now we can see that the plot was designed indirectly also *for* Angelo. The Duke manipulated and deceived Angelo the 'fallen Angel' in order to save Angelo the Man. At the end of the great apocalyptic scene (in so far as apocalypse is 'revelation'), Angelo's repentance is seen to be genuine. Therefore his pardon and forgiveness fulfill the scheme of atonement, or at-one-ment. But it is not only Angelo who is changed. There is room for improvement even in the life of saints. We have seen Isabella's immaturity, for all her high ideals and sanctity. Though in theory she was eloquently defending her integrity, nevertheless under the strain of events she went as far as saying that she would pray a thousand prayers for Claudio's death. But the greatest scene of the drama comes when she, supposing that Angelo has executed Claudio, is willing to kneel and plead for Angelo's life for Mariana's sake. As Northrop Frye says: 'As soon as she makes this speech we understand that this is really what the whole second half of the play has been about. The primary end and aim of everything the Duke is doing is to get that speech out of her.'[26] Both Angelo and Isabella are reformed characters by the end. Now we begin to see what all the fuss was about, although the Duke's marriage-proposal to Isabella may still strike us as strange. We naturally ask: how could Isabella accept the proposal when, until that moment, she has been so convinced of her vocation? To solve this enigma and arrive at a conclusion we need to know something about the comic form.

Nevil Coghill has shown that there existed in the sixteenth century two opposed views of comedy. The first one was the medieval view as defined by Vincent de Beauvais:

Et autem comoedia poesis, exordium triste, laeto commutans.

This view, namely that comedy starts in trouble and ends in joy was shared by Dante (as manifested in the *Divine Comedy*), by Chaucer and Lydgate and in almost every instance, by Shakespeare too. The other tradition may be defined in the words of Sir Philip Sidney: 'Comedy is an imitation of the common errors of our life'. This tradition was favoured by Ben Jonson.[27]

Shakespeare drew on the Dantean sense of the divine comedy as a reflection of the ultimate reality; the comic form is also a cosmic form.[28] Now in the Dantean form there is certainly a narrative pattern which begins in trouble and ends in joy and this is usually epitomized by the solemnity of the marriages.

Measure for Measure has been read as an allegory of a morality play, but Coghill takes issue with this viewpoint, placing the play in the older tradition of the parables just as Wilson Knight did. This means that the setting of the play is seen to be fully within the orbit of human affairs, but it puts the human situation into an eternal context. As we have said above, the persuasiveness of the narrative is not lost by the figuration. The classic example of this type of parabolic representation is Chaucer's *The Clerk's Tale*, from the *Canterbury Tales*. Like the *The Clerk's Tale*, *Measure for Measure* is also a parable of testing. Everybody is tested and measured in this play with the exception of Lucio. Coghill's argument that Lucio has known throughout that the Duke and the Friar are the same ('I know what I know') is intriguing if not entirely convincing. But perhaps in this comic and cosmic universe we may say that Lucio can be seen as the ironical counterpoint, the comic adversary, the eternal slanderer, the diabolos, the Satan of the Book of Job.

To sum up: *Measure for Measure* is constructed on the medieval pattern of comedy, the play ends with an image of *Paradiso*. But while, in the earlier comedies, the conflicts were due to misunderstanding, mistaken identity, shrewishness, in *Measure for Measure* the point of departure is the evil in human nature. Nevertheless, Shakespeare does not allow that evil has to end in tragedy. We live in a fallen world, yet there is hope for salvation, and thus the play, in Coghill's words, is the parable of man's salvation, the comedy of Adam.[29]

We have commented on three figurative readings of the play. Each of them preserves the sense of the play as play and not as an allegorical expression of some Christian sentiments but each of them justifies the reading of the play as a parable because of its inherent surplus of meaning and figurative drive. To conclude our discussion, we must say something about the ending of the play.

To many readers the ending of the play in which the Duke proposes marriage to Isabella, seems to be most problematic. Here we are confronted with what I would call the 'reality-fallacy'. Most readers who condemn Isabella and are irritated by the Duke, fall into this trap. They read the play as if it reflects 'real life'. But if we accept that there is magic in this play, even if of a prosaic kind, then we realize that we have to do with tales and the telling of tales rather than with a 'real-life' story. In this case our literal-mindedness will be shattered and there will be nothing to be surprised at. Shakespeare was not simply composing a comedy but also writing a 'meta-comedy', a comedy about the comedy, a self-reflection of the medieval convention of comedy.

Some perceptive directors of the play have been able to make sense of the ending of the play, while readers seeking a realistic conclusion have been disappointed. Desmond Davis, the director of *Measure for Measure* in the BBC Television series of Shakespeare's plays, so organized the setting of the entrance of the Duke in Act V Scene 1 that it gives the impression of a rehearsal of a performance on an Elizabethan stage. The people around the throne in the middle of the stage act as if they are part of an audience. The Duke takes the part of director demonstrating to the audience the meaning of the play. Here the function of the Duke is close to that of the Expositor in the Chester play, yet not wholly an extradramatic, but rather a metadramatic figure. How does the Duke's proposal of marriage to Isabella make sense in this context? One can read it also as the meta-dramatic culmination of the figurative interpretation: the Bridegroom (Christ) encounters his white-robed Bride (the Church) who has suffered much tribulation. But one can read it also as the director did: in Davis' production the Duke or the Deputy Director (acted by Kenneth Colley) makes his proposal to Isabella (Kate Nelligan). The cameraman shows Isabella for a while. She does not immediately react. In the silence tension grows. Isabella waits. She does not appear to be astonished or even surprised – her face is expressionless. Then, all of a sudden, for almost the first time in the play, there is a smile on her face, and she yields to the Duke as if she were obeying her director's final advice, saying something like 'Why not, if it is the end of the game?' This gesture supports the notion that we are 'out of the play'. Isabella accepts the arm of the Duke and they leave the stage cheerfully accompanied by the enthusiastic applause of the audience.

This '*Paradiso*-scene' conveys the impression of arriving at spiritual freedom after exciting, if exhausting labour. The tragic downward spiral of events has been miraculously reversed in the middle of the play. The law that was the enemy of human beings in the first half of the play 'has not been annulled or contradicted, but transcended; not broken but fulfilled by being internalized.'[30] The characters, the actors and even the audience now come to a liberating fulfilment. The play, in the sense of the Gospel, has indeed 'fulfilled its measure' (cf. Matthew 23:32).

FULFILMENT OF THE 'ETERNAL DESIGN' IN T. S. ELIOT'S *MURDER IN THE CATHEDRAL*

Our last case study is a twentieth-century poetic drama. Eliot's play serves as an excellent illustration of figurative interpretation for at least two reasons. First, the drama is not simply about martyrdom, but about the re-enacting of the 'pattern' of martyrdom. Becket is an antitype who fulfills the type of the protomartyr St Stephen (Acts 7), who had fulfilled the martyrdom of Christ. The play reflects this drive and advance towards fulfilment. There is a tension throughout the play and it is removed only when the design is fulfilled, 'When the figure of God's purpose is made complete'. Though at first we might consider the drama as a tragedy, at the end the chorus (that acknowledge themselves as 'type of the common man') is singing the *Te Deum* about the earth which is renewed by the blood of the martyrs. By the end it is obvious that the real shape of the play has to do much more with a Dantean sense of 'divine' comedy rather than with tragedy. Comedy is the genre of inclusion and fulfilment, while tragedy is the genre of exclusion and loss. Thus speaks Thomas before encountering his murderers:

> all things
> Proceed to a joyful consummation

We shall see that in the second half of the play the reader or the spectator is also meant to take part and become involved. So the genre is meant to fulfil the comic pattern and thus the play is about the fulfilment of the design and the realization of the pattern. Secondly, and in a way similar both to the Chester play of Abraham and to Shakespeare's *Measure for Measure*, typology or figuration implies also the conscious self-reflection of the genre: the 'pattern' is reinterpreted and thereby recreated. *Murder in the Cathedral* also contains meta-dramatic elements. At the end of the play for example, the reader or spectator is defamiliarized by the Knights' prosaic comments on their acts. As Eliot wrote in his essay on 'Poetry and Drama', the Knights' speeches are meant 'to shock the audience out of their complacency'.[31] The audience is asked to reflect upon what they have just witnessed. However, the function of the Knights is to be seen rather as parody or, as an inversion of the function performed by the Expositor or the Duke. They are not interpreters but misinterpreters. They are meant not only to deceive but to demoralize the audience, to confuse their sense of values or moral judgment. We shall see that they have a function in the symmetrical, typological pattern of the play itself.

Murder in the Cathedral is a verse drama which was written for the Canterbury Festival in June, 1935. The play itself is an interesting experiment, joining elements of the classical Greek tragedy with the traditions of the medieval mystery and morality plays. In his essay on 'Poetry and Drama', Eliot explains that he had to find a neutral style, committed neither to the present nor to the past. He had the versification of *Everyman* in his mind, which he deliberately broke with occasional, unusual rhymes or with a different rhythm. These conscious 'defamiliarizing' and 'decontextualizing' effects, together with the unexpected references to the 'English Essay', the 'children's party', 'the scholar's degree', were meant to shake the historical sense of the audience and their false sense of reality: 'Man's life is cheat and disappointment'. The meta-dramatic culmination of the play is anticipated by such meta-poetic effects: Eliot, just like the Duke, disorients his audience in order to reorient them. The invention of the chorus, representing the uncertain feelings of the ordinary people of Canterbury, provides a constant musical tone to the drama, just as their recurring allusions to the rotation of the seasonal cycle gives a sense of permanent rhythm to the play.

Reviving the tradition of medieval drama, the play is not only meant to delight but also instruct us in the meaning of martyrdom. The play is about the fulfilling of the 'pattern' of martyrdom which is said to be an 'eternal design'. We must not forget that medieval typologists spoke about the 'art' of God who designs his 'model' or 'mould' which will have to be filled in, in due course. Thus 'the art of martyrdom' is also a pattern that one has to recognize, adapt and thereby fulfill. But not everybody is meant for martyrdom. It is a call to be obeyed only by the elect. But martyrdom makes sense only if its significance is recognized by the community and this community can be regenerated by the blood of such martyrs. We shall see that the community also has a role in the eternal design of martyrdom and has equally to fulfill its own role in this design.

The play's structure is symmetrical: part one leads up to the interlude (Becket's Christmas sermon) and part two leads up to the Knights' rational justification of their murder. In both cases poetry leads up to prose. The first part is concerned with the eternal conflict taking place in Thomas' mind and the second part is about the external consequences of the internal conflict. The first part is characterized by 'suffering is action' and the second part by 'action is suffering'. Becket is prepared to be confronted with the tempters:

> Meanwhile the substance of our first act
> Will be shadows, and the strife with shadows.
> Heavier the interval than the consummation.
> All things prepare the event. Watch.

The first tempter reminds him of his happy, easy-going irresponsible youth, the second one invites him back to political life ('power is present holiness hereafter'). The third tempter appeals to the idea of the coalition with the barons, namely that the Normans should stick together. Thomas can easily refute these shadows. However, he was not expecting the fourth tempter. To his astonishment this last figure is tempting him with his own thoughts: he appeals to Thomas' own hidden vanity by suggesting he prepare for martyrdom because 'Saint and Martyr rule from the tomb'; the spiritual power is above the temporal glory. Becket's victory over the last tempter is the victory over the last ruins of almost completely collapsed ego. But he reaches perfection in his readiness for martyrdom only by overcoming this last temptation and by acknowledging that

> The last temptation is the greatest treason
> To do the right deed for the wrong reason.

He could easily have fallen even at this last stage on the journey to perfection, since the higher we are in our spiritual development, the lower we may fall. Becket had managed in the past to ascend in perfection and in his overcoming the first three temptations the reader may identify Kierkegaard's notion of the three stages: aesthetic, ethical and religious. But now the final test is the temptation of his own religion. And Becket, though not easily, could overcome even this last temptation. Only by this victory is he qualified ripe and ready for martyrdom. This liberating experience leads him to say:

> I know
> What yet remains to show you of my history
> Will seem to most of you at best futility,
> Senseless self-slaughter of a lunatic,
> Arrogant passion of a fanatic.

However, before the completion of his suffering *in* action he delivers his Christmas sermon to the people of Canterbury. The prose-sermon is delivered 'after he has overcome the conflict in his mind and is awaiting martyrdom . . . [this] is the voice of reason accommodating revelation to human ears'.[32] At Christmas, on St Stephen's Day, Becket, having the example of the first Christian martyr and the reality of his own impending martyrdom in mind, is authorized by God to teach about the true meaning of martyrdom:

> A Christian martyrdom is never an accident, for Saints are not made by accident. Still less is a Christian martyrdom the effect of a man's will to become a Saint, as a man by willing and contriving may become a ruler of men. A martyrdom is always the design of God, for his love of men, to warn them, to lead them, to bring them back to His ways. It is never the design of man; for the true martyr is he who has become the instrument of God, for His love of men, to warn them and to lead them, to bring them back to his ways. It is never the design of men; for the true martyr is he who has lost his will in the will of God, and who no longer desires anything for himself, not even the glory of being a martyr.

David E. Jones rightly observed that in the drama 'Historical detail is severely subordinated to the pattern or design of martyrdom which gives the play its shape as well as its meaning'.[33] The action of the second part is indeed only the inaction or completion of suffering. The impending disaster is at hand: the priests are afraid of being left alone, the chorus sings about void and emptiness and the beast-like Knights arrive to mock Thomas as Daniel: 'Are you washed in the blood of the Lamb?' But Becket is aware of the meaning of the blood:

> This is the sign of the church always,
> The sign of blood. Blood for blood.
> His blood given to buy my life,
> My blood given to pay for His death,
> My death for His death.

The murder is carried out followed by the lamentation of the chorus: 'Clear the air ! clean the sky ! wash the wind ! . . . '

At this point the play turns into a meta-drama: the Knights 'step out' of the context of the play with the purpose of addressing the twentieth-century audience. These knights, unlike the anonymous priests or the chorus have their own individual names and they try to provide a rational justification of their murder. Their language is a rational, discursive one that Northrop Frye would probably identify with the third, descriptive phase of language and with causal thinking. This harsh tone appears as a sharp contrast to the poetry and the musicality of the play as a whole. We find their arguments, especially their political ones, at times quite convincing: the kingdom was divided and the king wanted to restore order and national unity. It is only when the fourth knight begins to explain that Becket was killed by his own egotism and yearning for glory, the 'Suicide of an Unsound Mind', that we begin to realize we have almost fallen into a trap, that we, the audience, are also being tempted. Now the typological structure of the whole drama becomes evident. It is not difficult to see the symmetrical similarity between the four tempters and the four knights, but in addition to the parallel construction we have to recognize that the four knights re-enact typologically the four successive temptations in the first part. Jones is right in emphasizing that the first half of the pattern of martyrdom is fulfilled by the martyr and the second is concerned with 'the creation of the attitude of acceptance in the great mass of believers'.[34]

The true martyrdom requires the fulfilment of two halves of a pattern. The first half must be fulfilled by the martyr himself; he must accept his martyrdom in the right spirit . . . But as martyrdom requires the right attitude on the part of the martyr, so also it requires the right attitude on the part of the great mass of men. A martyrdom is not efficacious unless it is accepted by them as 'the design of God . . .'[35]

Just as the martyr had to obey 'the designer', so the community has to accept the spirit of this design. The community that is prone to forget must continually be reminded and instructed afresh in the meaning of the pattern of martyrdom because in due course they may have to repeat the pattern. Like Thomas, the audience has to resist a series of temptations, first of all the temptation of rationality, discursive logic and the nature of the exclusively political argument. But once they have overcome the temptation the pattern is absorbed and fixed within them. With 'the book swallowed', the audience becomes involved in and embraced by the 'eternal design'. This is obvious at the end, when the audience is converted into a congregation, praising and affirming the glory of the creator God.

When the pattern is eventually completed, when the figure comes to fulfilment, the uneasy process of events comes to a standstill. Here we find ourselves surprized by order after the experience of chaos. As Eliot put it in his essay: 'it is ultimately the function of art in imposing a credible order upon ordinary reality, to bring us to a condition of serenity, stillness and reconciliation.'[36]

CONCLUSION: THE FIGURE FULFILLED

We have arrived at the final conclusion or the destination of our journey. Our purpose was to establish a theory of typology on the basis of reader-response criticism. Typology is an experience of fulfilment and it is provoked by the 'fulfilment-language' of the Bible. Typology and fulfilment are realized in the act of reading. We have read some texts of Scripture that were reading other texts. We have read pictures that were conscious of the intertextual interplay of prefiguration and fulfilment. In our last chapter we have read literature that adopted the figurative mode.

Each of the three dramas we were concerned with were hermeneutical plays. In each of them there was a surplus of meaning and each play was partly about interpretation. In each of them there was pattern or design, whether it was the pattern of the Crucifixion, the pattern of the divine comedy, or the pattern of martyrdom. The dramatists' concern was not only to uphold this pattern but to fulfill it. Obedience, like imitation (in the sense of *Imitatio Christi*), is crucial to the success of fulfilment. Only by obeying the language and respecting the pattern can we recreate the pattern. In Eliot's words: 'only in time can time be conquered'. The rhythm must be kept. But just as typology defamiliarizes our conventional use of language, these plays also shock us out of our complacency with regard to our experience of drama or dramatic form. We find ourselves disoriented by the unexpected figure of the Expositor, by the deceiving games of Duke Vincentio and by the Knights' interpretation of their murder. But the ultimate purpose, the aim of the game, is reorientation by disorientation, the recreation, or the fulfilling of the pattern.

To achieve this, typology in all the three plays creates a meta-drama. Typology is itself a meta-language as by means of typology our experience of language is lifted up into a higher reality. Just as *Steigerung* is a leap both upward and forward, meta-drama lifts us onto a higher plane insofar as it creates a reality where drama can reflect upon itself. Comedy is a particularly appropriate form for meta-drama as it has an inherent drive towards fulfilment.

Meta-comedy that creates this higher sense of reality by means of typology is able now to absorb the reader or the audience into its world. Unlike tragedy that aims at 'holding up a mirror to nature', the meta-comedy makes us a part of the play. We are not complacent spectators any more, we are involved in the drama. Through the act of reading we have become witnesses of what is taking place in the great cosmic stage of the world. Reading is testimony.

Notes

1: Introduction

1. Northrop Frye, *The Great Code: The Bible and Literature* (London: Routledge & Kegan Paul, 1982)
2. Erich Auerbach, 'Figura' in *Scenes from the Drama of European Literature*, trans. R. Mannheim (New York: Meridian, 1959) pp. 11–74; *Typologische Motive in der mittelalterlichen Literatur* (1953); 'Typological Symbolism in Medieval Literature', in *Yale French Studies* (New York, 1965):3–10; *Mimesis: The Representation of Reality in Western Literature* (Princeton: Princeton University Press, 1971); A. C. Charity, *Events and Their Afterlife: the Dialectics of Christian Typology in the Bible and Dante* (Cambridge: Cambridge University Press, 1966); Barbara Kiefer Lewalski, *Protestant Poetics and Seventeenth Century Religious Lyric* (Princeton: Princeton University Press, 1979); William G. Madsen, *From Shadowy Types to Truth: Studies in Milton's Symbolism* (New Haven: Yale University Press, 1980); Frank Kermode, *The Genesis of Secrecy* (Cambridge, Mass.: Harvard University Press, 1974); George P. Landow, *Victorian Types, Victorian Shadows: Biblical Typology in Victorian Literature, Art and Thought* (London: Routledge and Kegan Paul, 1980), *William Holmann Hunt and Typological Symbolism* (New Haven: Yale University Press, 1979); Paul J. Korshin, *Typologies in England 1650–1820* (Princeton: Princeton University Press, 1982).
3. Friedrich Ohly, 'Vom Geistigen Sinn des Wortes in Mittelalter', in *Schriften zur Mittelalterlichen Bedeutungsforschung* (Darmstadt: Wissenschaftliche Buchgesellschaft, 1977):1–31. First published in *Zeitschrift fur deutsches Altertum und deutsche Literatur*, 89 (1958–59):1–23; 'Synagoge und Ecclesia. Typologisches im mittelalterlicher Dichtung', in *Schriften...*, pp. 312–37; 'Halbbiblische und ausserbiblische Typologie' in *Schriften...*, pp. 361–99; *Gesetz und Evangelium: zur Typologie bei Luther und Lucas Cranach. Zum Blutstrahl der Gnade in der Kunst* (Munster: Aschendorf, 1985).
4. Perry Miller, *Errand into the Wilderness* (Cambridge, Mass.: Belknap Press, 1956); Ursula Brumm, *American Thought and Religious Typology* (New Brunswick: Rutgers, University Press, 1970); Sacvan Bercovitch (ed.), *Typology and Early American Literature* (Amherst, Mass., 1972); Sacvan Bercovitch (ed.), *The American Puritan Imagination* (Cambridge: Cambridge University Press, 1974), *The Puritan Origins of The American Self* (New Haven:

Yale University Press, 1975), *The American Jeremiad* (Madison: University of Wisconsin Press, 1978); Mason I. Lowance, *The Language of Canaan: Metaphor and Symbol in New England from the Puritans to the Transcendentalists* (Cambridge, Mass.: Harvard University Press, 1980).
5. P. Joseph Cahill's review of *Creation and Recreation* in *Studies in Religion: Science religieuse* 10 (1981) 235-6
6. *The Great Code*, p. xiv.
7. John Ayre, *Northrop Frye: A Biography* (Toronto: Random House, 1989) p. 109.
8. *The Great Code*, p. xvii.
9. Northrop Frye, *Anatomy of Criticism Four Essays* (New Jersey: Princeton University Press, 1957)
10. Ibid., p. 315.
11. Ibid., p. 191.
12. *The Great Code*, p. 78.
13. Ibid., p. 78.
14. Ibid., p. 27.
15. Ibid., p. 29.
16. Paul Ricoeur, 'What is a Text?', in David Klemm (ed.), *The Hermeneutical Inquiry*, Vol. 1 (Atlanta, Georgia: Scholars Press, 1986, pp. 233-45).
17. *The Great Code*, p. 106.
18. Ibid. p. 138.
19. Ibid., p. 86.
20. P. Joseph Cahill, 'The Unity of the Bible', in *Biblica*, 65 (1984): 406.
21. Ibid., p. 407.
22. Ibid., p. 409.
23. Brevard S. Childs, 'The *Sensus Literalis*' of Scripture: An Ancient and Modern Problem', in H. Donner, R. Hanhart, R. Smend (eds), *Beitrage zur Alttestamentliche Theologie: FS Walter Zimmerli* (Göttingen: Vanhock and Ruprecht, 1977), pp. 80-99.
24. Gerald T. Sheppard, *The Future of the Bible: Beyond Literalism and Liberalism* (Toronto: United Church Publishing House, 1990), p. 29.
25. A frequently recurring notion in Paul Ricoeur's writings, especially in *Symbolism of Evil* (Boston: Beacon Press, 1967); and in *The Conflict of Interpretations: Essays in Hermeneutics* (Evanston, Ill.: Northwestern University Press, 1974), pp. 269-86.
26. The quotations are conflated from various writings of Harold Bloom cited in the notes of Linda Munk's manuscript: 'The Seamless Garment: for Northrop Frye', forthcoming in *The University of Toronto Quarterly*. I am most grateful to Dr Linda Munk for passing her manuscript for me.
27. J. R. Darbyshire, 'Typology', in *Encyclopedia of Religion and Ethics*,

Vol. XIX (Edinburgh, 1921), pp. 503-4.
28. Leonard Goppelt, *Die typologische Deutung des Alten Testaments in Neuen* (Gutersloh, 1939). The second enlarged edition was published in 1969. The English translation was published in 1982: *Typos: The Typological Interpretation of the Old Testament in the New*, trans. D. Madvig (Michigan: W. B. Eerdmans, 1982).
29. Rudolf Bultmann, 'Urprung und Sinn der Typologie als hermeneutischer Methode', in *Theologische Literaturzeitung*, 75 (1950): 205-12.

2: The Hermeneutical Context

1. *The Great Code*, pp. 29-30.
2. Ibid.
3. Frye's forthcoming book (a sequel to *The Great Code*) will be entitled *Words With Power*. John Ayre suggests (*Northrop Frye: A Biography*, p. 385) that Frye made a crucial change in the preposition. Instead of the originally intended title *Words Of Power* he chose the title *Words With Power* as an allusion to Luke 4:32 mainly because the former version evokes magic which he definitely rejects. Anthony C. Thisleton also warns us against ideas 'word-magic' in 'The Supposed Power of Words in the Biblical Writings', *The Journal of Theological Studies*, XXV (1974): 283-99.
4. Auerbach, *Mimesis*, pp. 14-5.
5. Northrop Frye, *Creation and Recreation* (Toronto: University of Toronto Press, 1980), p. 65.
6. Ricoeur, *Symbolism of Evil*, p. 349; italics mine.
7. Paul Ricoeur, *Freud and Philosophy: an Essay on Interpretation* (New Haven: Yale University Press, 1970) p. 31.
8. Ibid.
9. Leonard Goppelt, 'Typos', in *Theological Dictionary of the New Testament*, ed. G. Friedrich (Michigan: W. B. Eerdmans, 1971), p. 53.
10. Cf. W. G. Madsen, '"Earth the Shadow of Heaven": Typological Symbolism in *Paradise Lost*', in *PMLA*, LXXV (1960): 519-26.
11. Frye, *Creation and Recreation*, p. 70.
12. C. F. D. Moule, 'Fulfil', in *The Interpreter's Dictionary of the Bible*, Vol. II (New York: Abingdon Press, 1962), p. 328. See also Moule's excellent article '"Fulness" and "Fill" in the New Testament', *Scottish Journal of Theology*, IV (1951): 79-86.
13. Brevard S. Childs, 'Prophecy and Fulfilment', in *Interpretation* Vol. XII (July 1958): 267.
14. Ibid.
15. Ricoeur, *Freud*, p. 9.
16. Auerbach, 'Figura', p. 53.

17. Goppelt, *Typos* (English edition, 1982), pp. 225–6.
18. R. E. Brown, 'Hermeneutics', in *Jerome Biblical Commentary*, ed. R. E. Brown, J. A. Fitzmeyer, R. E. Murphy (London: Geoffrey Chapman, 1968) p. 616–8.
19. Origen, 'On First Principle: Book Four', in Karlfried Froehlich, *Biblical Interpretation in the Early Church* (Philadelphia: Fortress Press, 1975), p. 59.
20. Harry Caplan, 'The Four Senses of Scripture Interpretation and the Medieval Theory of Preaching' in *Speculum*, 4 (1929): 286. Cf. J. Cassian, *Collatio* XIV, 8 PL 49, p. 963. In English: *Conferences* (New York: Paulist Press, 1985).
21. Childs, '*Sensus Literalis* . . . ', op. cit. p. 92.
22. Frye, *The Great Code*, p. 45.
23. Ibid., p. 60.
24. Ibid., p. 61.
25. Ibid., p. 220.
26. Ibid., p. 221.
27. Origen, 'On First Principle', in Froehlich, p. 59.
28. Quoted by Robert M. Grant, *A Short History of the Interpretation of the Bible* (New York: Macmillan, 1963; rev. edn), p. 91.
29. Diodore of Tarsus, 'Commentary on the Psalms: Prologue', in Froehlich, op. cit., p. 83
30. Ibid. p. 85–6.
31. Ibid. p. 93.
32. Herman Hailperin, *Rashi and the Christian Scholars* (Pittsburgh: University of Pittsburgh Press, 1963), p. 107.
33. Quoted by Beryl Smalley, *The Study of the Bible in the Middle Ages*, (Oxford: Oxford University Press, 1941), p. 100.
34. Quoted ibid., p. 87.
35. Jeremy Taylor (ed. and trans.), *The Didascalicon of Hugh of St Victor* (New York and London: Columbia University Press, 1961), p. 138.
36. Ibid., p. 149.
37. Ibid., p. 150.
38. Ibid., p. 150. Augustine, *De genesi ad litteram*, I. XVIII (PL. XXIV)
39. R. E. Brown, *The Sensus Plenior of Sacred Scripture* (Baltimore: St Mary's University, 1955). 'The *Sensus Plenior* in the Last Ten Years', in *Catholic Biblical Commentary* 25 (1963): 262–85; 'The Problems of the *Sensus Plenior*' in *Bibliotheca Ephemeridium Theologicarum Lovaniensium*, 26 (1968); 'Hermeneutics', in *Jerome Biblical Commentary*, op. cit., p. 617.
40. Robert Bruce Robinson, *Roman Catholic Exegesis Since 'Divino Afflante Spiritu'* (Georgia: Scholars Press, 1982), p. 30.
41. R. E. Brown, *The Sensus Plenior of Sacred Scripture*, p. 92
42. R. E. Brown, 'The Problems . . . ' op. cit. (1968), p. 72.
43. R. E. Brown, *The Sensus Plenior of Sacred Scripture*, p. 145.

44. R. E. Brown, *Jerome Biblical Commentary*, p. 617.
45. R. B. Robinson, *Roman Catholic Exegesis Since "Divino Afflante Spiritu"*. In 1981 Brown retrospectedly wrote about his early interest in the SP: 'the hermeneutical stress I advocated was too narrowly scholastic and tied into the principle of single authorship for a biblical book.' R. E. Brown, *The Critical Meaning of the Bible* (New York: Paulist Press, 1981), p. 29
46. J. M. Robinson, 'Scripture and Theological Method: a Protestant Study in *Sensus Plenior*' in *Catholic Biblical Quarterly*, 27 (1965): 6–27.
47. William Sanford LaSor, 'Prophecy, Inspiration and *Sensus Plenior*', in *Tyndale Bulletin*, 29 (1978): 50.
48. Ibid., 55.
49. Ibid., 51.
50. Ibid.
51. Ibid. 57.
52. Ibid., 60; italics mine. See also William Sanford LaSor, 'The *Sensus Plenior* and Biblical Interpretation', in W. W. Gasque, W. S. LaSor (eds), *Scripture Tradition and Interpretation* (Michigan: W. B. Eerdmans, 1978); Douglas J. Moo, 'The Problem of the *Sensus Plenior*', in D. A. Carson, J. D. Woodbridge (eds), *Hermeneutics Authority and Canon* (Grand Rapids: Zondervan, 1986), p. 202.
53. Douglas A. Oss, 'Canon as Context: The Function of *Sensus Plenior* in Evangelical Hermeneutics', in *Grace Theological Journal*, 9.1 (1988): 105.
54. Walter Vogels, 'Inspiration in a Linguistic Mode', in *Biblical Theological Bulletin*, 15 (1985): 87–93.
55. Ibid., 88.
56. Ibid., 89.
57. Ibid.
58. Ibid. 90.
59. Ibid.
60. Ricoeur, 'What is a Text?', in Klemm (ed.), *The Hermeneutical Inquiry*, Vol. 1, pp. 233–45).
61. Ibid.
62. Paul Ricoeur, *Interpretation Theory* (Texas: Texas Christian University Press, 1976), p. 94.
63. Frye, *The Great Code*, p. 138.
64. Auerbach, *Mimesis*, pp. 14–15.
65. Quoted by Frye in *The Great Code*, p. 138.

3: Reading Scripture

1. Frye quoted by P. J. Cahill, 'The Unity of the Bible', in *Biblica* 65 (1984): 404.

2. Oscar Cullmann, *Salvation in History* (London: SCM, 1967), p. 132 (the German original is from 1965).
3. Ibid., p. 249.
4. B. Anderson, 'Exodus Typology in Second Isaiah', in *Israel's Prophetic Heritage* (London: SCM, 1962), p. 90.
5. Gerhard von Rad, 'Typologische Auslegung des Alten Testaments', in *Evangelische Theologie*, 12 (1952): 17–33. In English: 'Typological Interpretation of the Old Testament', trans. John Bright, in *Essays in Old Testament Hermeneutics* ed. Claus Waterman (Richmond: John Knox Press, 1963), pp. 17–39.
6. Gerhard von Rad, *Theologie des alten Testaments* II (Munchen, Kaiser, 1960) pp. 17–39. English translation: *Old Testament Theology*, Vol. II, *Israel's Prophetic Traditions* (Edinburgh: Oliver and Boyd, 1965).
7. von Rad, *Essays in Old Testament Hermeneutics*, p. 17
8. von Rad, *Israel's Prophetic Traditions*, p. 358.
9. von Rad, *Essays in Old Testament Hermeneutics*, p. 39.
10. Ibid., p. 36.
11. John H. Stek, 'Biblical Typology Yesterday and Today', in *Calvin Theological Journal*, 5 (1970): 152.
12. Ibid., 142.
13. Michael Fishbane, *Biblical Interpretation in Ancient Israel* (Oxford: Clarendon Press, 1985), pp. 350–79.
14. Ibid.
15. Ibid. p. 372–3.
16. Robert Alter, *The Art of Biblical Narrative* (New York: Basic Book Publishers, 1981), p. 50.
17. Northrop Frye, *The Bible and Literature*: A Personal View from Northrop Frye (Toronto: Media Center, University of Toronto, 1982–3). Thirty colour video programs with manuals. Executive Producer: Bob Rogers. Lecture 15: 'The Question of Primogeniture'.
18. Fishbane, *Biblical Interpretation in Ancient Israel*, p. 358.
19. Charity, *Events and Their Afterlife: the Dialectics of Christian Typology in the Bible and Dante*, p. 39.
20. Ibid.
21. Ibid. p. 76.
22. Fishbane, *Biblical Interpretation in Ancient Israel*, p. 356.
23. Ibid.
24. Cf. Note 4.
25. Horace Hummel, 'The Old Testament Basis of Typological Interpretation', in *Biblical Research*, IX (1964): 41.
26. Ibid., 48.
27. Charity, *Events and Their Afterlife: the Dialectics of Christian Typology in the Bible and Dante*, p. 148–64.
28. See, for example, A. J. Maas, *Christ in Type and Prophecy* (New

York: Chicago, Beuzinger Brothers, 1896) Vol. II, p. 335.
29. Goppelt, *Typos*, p. 66.
30. Ibid., p. 67. Quoted by Goppelt from Schniewind.
31. Ibid.
32. Ibid., p. 90.
33. Ibid., p. 92.
34. Ibid., p. 94.
35. Ricoeur, *Symbolism of Evil*, p. 260-78.
36. Goppelt, *Typos*, p. 105.
37. Ricoeur, *Symbolism of Evil*, p. 271.
38. Goppelt, *Typos*, p. 112.
39. Ibid., p. 114.
40. Ibid., p. 180.
41. Ibid., p. 182.
42. Ibid., p. 190.
43. Ibid., p. 191.
44. M. D. Goulder, *Type and History in Acts* (London: SPCK, 1964)
45. E. Earle Ellis, *Paul's Use of the Old Testament* (Edinburgh: Oliver and Boyd, 1957), p. 128.
46. Goppelt, *Typos*, p. 129.
47. Ibid., p. 132. Goppelt quotes from A. Oepke.
48. Ibid., p. 138.
49. On the 'rock' in Victorian literature see G. P. Landow, *Victorian Types*, pp. 65-94.
50. Goppelt, *Typos*, p. 223.
51. *The Shorter Oxford English Dictionary*, Vol. II (Oxford: Clarendon Press, 1973). p. 2348.
52. Frye, *Bible and Literature*, Lecture 28: 6.
53. Frye, *The Great Code*, p. 226.
54. Ibid., p. 138.
55. Ibid.

4: Reading Pictures

1. Walter Ong, *The Presence of the Word* (New Haven and London: Yale University Press, 1967); *Orality and Literacy* (London and New York: Methuen, 1982)
2. Walter Ong, 'Text As Interpretation: Mark and After', in *Semeia* 39 (1987): 9.
3. Clifford Davidson, 'The Anti-Visual Prejudice' in *Iconoclasm Vs. Art and Drama*, ed. Clifford Davidson and Ann Eljenholm Nichols, *Early Drama, Art and Music Monograph Series*, 11 (Kalamazoo, Michigan: Medieval Institute Publications, 1989), pp. 33-4.
4. Joseph Gutmann, 'Deotoronomy: Religious Reform or Iconoclastic Revolution?' in *The Image and the Word: Confrontations in*

Judaism, Christianity and Islam, ed. Joseph Gutmann (Missoula: Scholars Press, 1977), pp. 5–25.
5. Jonas Barish, *The Anti-Theatrical Prejudice* (Berkely and Los Angeles: University of California Press, 1981).
6. Cf. Anthony Bryer and Judith Herrin (eds), *Iconoclasm*, Papers Given at the Ninth Spring Symposion of Byzantine Studies, 1975 (Birmingham: Centre for Byzantine Studies, 1977); Stephen Gero, 'Byzantine Iconoclasm and the failure of a Medieval Reformation' in Gutmann (ed.), *The Image and the Word*, pp. 49–62.
7. Quoted by William R. Jones, 'Art and Christian Piety: Iconoclasm in Medieval Europe', in Gutmann (ed.), *The Image and the Word*, p. 79.
8. Ibid., p. 81, and Anthony Ugolnik, 'The *Libri Carolini*: Antecedents of Reformation Iconoclasm', in Davidson (ed.), *Iconoclasm*, pp. 1–32.
9. Quoted by Margaret R. Miles, *Image as Insight: Visual Understanding in Western Christianity* (Boston: Beacon Press, 1985), p. 41.
10. Quoted ibid., p. 95
11. Quoted ibid., p. 152.
12. Quoted, ibid., p. 101.
13. Ibid.
14. Quoted by Ernest B. Gilman, *Iconoclasm and Poetry in the English Reformation: Down Went Dagon* (Chicago and London: University of Chicago Press, 1986), p. 36. The quotation is without reference.
15. Ibid. p. 34. and p. 201.
16. Carl C. Christensen, *Art and Reformation in Germany* (Athens, Ohio: Ohio State University Press, 1979), p. 25.
17. Miles, *Image as Insight: Visual Understanding in Western Christianity*, pp. 102–8.
18. Ibid., p. 108. See also, C. Garside, *Zwingli and the Arts* (New Haven: Yale University Press, 1966)
19. Quoted by Christensen, *Art and Reformation in Germany*, p. 42.
20. Quoted ibid., p. 45.
21. Quoted ibid., p. 49.
22. Cf. Miles, *Image as Insight: Visual Understanding in Western Christianity*, p. 117.
23. Quoted by Gilman, *Iconoclasm and Poetry in the English Reformation: Down Went Dagon*, p. 35.
24. Miles, *Image as Insight: Visual Understanding in Western Christianity*, p. 12
25. Ibid., p. 27.
26. Ibid., p. 39. and p. 35.
27. Ibid. p. 151.
28. Anna C. Esmeijer, *Divina Quaternitatis: A Preliminary Study in the Method and Application of Visual Exegesis* (Amsterdam: Van

Gorcum Assen, 1978), p. ix. See also a lenghty critical review of the book by Anton Van Run, in *Simiolus* 12 (1981–82): 70–77.
29. Ibid., 2.
30. Cf. Peter Bloch, 'Typologische Kunst', in *Miscellana Mediaevalia 6: Lex et Sacramntum in Mittelalter*, ed. P. Wilpert (Berlin: Walter de Gruyter & Comp., 1969), pp. 127–42.
31. *PL* 83: 97–130.
32. M. R. James, 'Pictor in Carmine', *Archeologia Society of Antiquarians of London*, Vol. XCIV (1951): 141–66. The quotation is p. 141.
33. Ibid., p. 143.
34. Ibid., p. 141–2.
35. Floridus Röhrig, '"Rota in medio rotae" Ein typologischer Zyklus aus Östereich', in *Jahrbuch des Stiftes Klosterneuburg*, Neue Folge, Band 5, pp. 7–113. On the various titles p. 35.
36. Esmeijer, *Divina Quaternitatis: A Preliminary Study in the Method and Application of Visual Exegesis*, p. 15.
37. Cf. Röhrig, '"Rota in medio rotae" Ein typologischer Zyklus aus Ostereich', p. 35–7
38. Röhrig, '"Rota in medio rotae" Ein typologischer Zyklus aus Ostereich', p. 33.
39. Floridus Röhrig, *Der Verduner Altar* (Klosterneuburg: Stift Klosterneuburg, 1984; 1st edn, 1955) See also Helmut Buschhausen, *Der Verduner Altar: das Emailwerk des Nikolaus von Verdun im Stift Klosterneuburg* (Wien: Tusch, 1980).
40. Rohrig, '"Rota in medio rotae" Ein typologischer Zyklus aus Ostereich', pp. 36–43.
41. Helmut Buschausen, 'The Theological Sources of the Klosterneuburg Altarpiece', in *The Year 1200: A Symposium*, Introduced by Geffrey Hoffeld (New York: The Metropolotan Museum of Arts, 1975), pp. 119–29. Quotation pp. 106. and 110.
42. Röhrig, *Der Verduner Altar*, p. 55.
43. Cf. Buschhausen, 'The Theological Sources of the Klosterneuburg Altarpiece'; see also, Helmut Buschhausen, 'The Klosterneuburg Altar of Nicholas of Verdun: Art, Theology and Politics', in *Journal of the Warburg and Courtauld Institutes*, XXXVII (1974): 1–31.
44. J. Sidney Groseclose, 'Discrete and Progressive Narration: Typology and Architechtonics of the Verdun Altar, *Auslegung of Paternostes* and the *Di Vier Schieven*' in *Studies in the Literary Imagination* (1975–76): viii-ix.
45. Quoted by Buschhausen, 'The Theological Sources of the Klosterneuburg Altarpiece', p. 112.
46. Ibid., p. 122.
47. Ibid., p. 124.
48. Cf. note 43.

49. Avril Henry (ed.), *Biblia Pauperum* (Aldershot: Scolar Press, 1987), p. 18.
50. Avril Henry, 'Biblia Pauperum', in *A Dictionary of Biblical Interpretation*, ed. R. J. Coggins, J. L. Houlden (London: SCM Press, 1990), p. 83.
51. Henry, *Biblia Pauperum*, p. 6.
52. Ibid., p. 16.
53. Eg.G. Schmidt, *Die Armenbibeln des XIV Jahrhunderts* (Graz: Köln, 1959).
54. Henry, 'Biblia Pauperum', p. 83.
55. Ibid.
56. Ibid.
57. Ibid.
58. Cf. Avril Henry (ed.), *The Mirour of Mans Saluacione: A Middle English translation of Speculum Humanae Salvationis* (Aldershot: Scolar Press, 1986), p. 10.
59. Adrian Wilson, Joyce Lancaster Wilson (eds), *A Medieval Mirror: Speculum humanae salvationis 1324–1500* (Berkeley, Los Angeles, London: The University of California Press, 1984). Quotation is from the cover-jacket.
60. Quoted by Emile Mâle, *Religious Art in France: The Late Middle Ages A Study of Medieval Iconography and Its Sources* (Princeton: Princeton University Press, 1986; (1st edn: 1908), p. 220.
61. Henry, *The Mirour of Mans Saluacione: A Middle English translation of Speculum Humanae Salvationis*, p. 10
62. Quoted by Mâle, *Religious Art in France: The Late Middle Ages A Study of Medieval Iconography and Its Sources*, p. 220.
63. Ibid., p. 221.
64. Henry, *The Mirour of Mans Saluacione: A Middle English translation of Speculum Humanae Salvationis*, p. 12.
65. Cf. note 58.
66. Mâle, *Religious Art in France: The Late Middle Ages A Study of Medieval Iconography and Its Sources*, p. 222.
67. Wilson, Wilson (eds), *A Medieval Mirror: Speculum humanae salvationis 1324–1500*, p. 136.
68. Henry, *Biblia Pauperum*, p. 66.
69. Wilson, Wilson (eds), *A Medieval Mirror: Speculum humanae salvationis 1324–1500*, p. 189.
70. Mâle, *Religious Art in France: The Late Middle Ages A Study of Medieval Iconography and Its Sources*, p. 227.
71. Emile Mâle, *Religous Art in France. The Thirteenth Century* (New Jersey: Princeton University Press), 1986. p. 145 ff.
72. Jean Paul Derembe, Colette Manhes, *Les vitreaux légendaires de Chartres* (Paris: Desche de Brouwer, 1988).
73. Ulrike Brinkmann, *Das jungere Bibelfenster* (Koln: Verlag Kolner Dom, s.d.).

74. See the short survey of Richard Marks' Dissertation, 'The Stained Glass of the Collegiate Church of Holy Trinity, Tattershall (Lincs.)' (London: 1975), pp. 191–3.
75. M. Cavinnes, *The Early Stained Glass of Canterbury Cathedral* (New Jersey: Princeton University Press, 1986.)
76. Henry, *Biblia Pauperum*, p. 37. See also Richard Marks, 'The Glazing of the Collegiate Church of the Holy Trinity, Tattershall (Linc.). A Study of Late Fifteen Century Glass-Painting Workshops', in *Archaeologia*, 106 (1979): 133–56.
77. Henry, *Biblia Pauperum*, p. 37.
78. H. Wayment, F. Wormall, *The Windows of King's College Chapel Cambridge: a Description and Commentary* (London: Oxford University Press, 1972); see especially pp. 5–9.
79. Michel Pomparet, *Les Tapisseries de L'Abbatiale Saint-Robert de Le Chaise-Dieu* (Brioude: Editions Watel, 1975).

5: Reading Literature

1. An English prose renderering sounds as follows:
   'Every created thing of the world/is like a book or a picture,/acting to us as a mirror,/a faithful figure,/ of our life, our death,/our condition, our lot' (cf. *PL* 210, 579a).
2. Quoted in Gabriel Josipovici, *The World and the Book: A Study in Modern Fiction* (London: Macmillan, 1971) p. 29.
3. Earl Miner (ed.), *Literary Uses of Typology from the Middle Ages to the Present* (Princeton: Princeton University Press, 1977).
4. Murray Roston, *Biblical Drama in England. From the Middle Ages to the Present Day* (London: Faber and Faber, 1968).
5. Ibid., pp. 70–1.
6. E. Auerbach, 'Figura', p. 53.
7. Ibid., pp. 71–2.
8. Stuart George Hall (ed.), *Melito of Sardis on Pascha and Fragments* (Oxford: Clarendon Press, 1973), p. 19.
9. V. A. Kolve, *The Play Called Corpus Christi* (London: Edward Arnold, 1966), p. 85.
10. Ibid., p. 72.
11. Rosemary Woolf, 'The Effect of Typology on the English Medieval Plays of Abraham and Isaac', in *Speculum*, 32 (1957): 805.
12. R. T. Davies (ed.), *The Corpus Christi Play of the English Middle Ages* (London: Faber and Faber, 1972), p. 417. This modernized edition contains the 'Ludus Conventriae' cycle and five other plays of Abraham and Isaac.
13. Ibid., p. 385.
14. David Bevington, *Medieval Drama* (Boston: Houghton Mifflin Company, 1975, p. 308.)
15. R. M. Lumiansky and David Mills (ed.), *The Chester Mystery*

Cycle, EETS, S. S. 3. (London: Oxford University Press, 1974), p. 62.
16. Peter W. Travis, *Dramatic Design in the Chester Cycle* (Chicago: The University of Chicago Press, 1982), pp. 80–1.
17. Northrop Frye, *The Myth of Deliverance* (Toronto: The University of Toronto Press, 1983.) p. 3.
18. Béla Hamvas, *Scientia Sacra: Az öskori emberiség szellemi hagyománya* (Budapest: Magvetö, 1988), p. 380.
19. G. Wilson Knight, 'Measure for Measure and the Gospels', in *The Wheel of Fire* (London: Oxford University Press, 1930).
20. Ibid., p. 82.
21. Ibid., p. 83.
22. Ibid., p. 106.
23. Paul Ricoeur, 'The "Kingdom" in the Parables of Jesus', in *Anglican Theological Review*, 63 (1981): 165–169.
24. Roy W. Battenhouse, 'Measure for Measure and the Christian Doctrine of the Atonement', in *PMLA*, 61 (1946): 1029–59.
25. On the Atonement cf. F. W. Dillistone, *The Christian Understanding of Atonement* (Digwell Place Welwyn: James Nisbet & Comp., 1968).
26. Frye, *Myth*, p. 29.
27. Nevil Coghill, 'Comic Form in Measure for Measure', in *Shakespeare Survey*, 8 (1955): pp. 14–27 at 17.
28. Ibid., p. 18.
29. Ibid., p. 26.
30. Frye, *Myth*, p. 30.
31. T. S. Eliot, 'Poetry and Drama', in *On Poetry and Poets* (London: Faber and Faber, 1957), p. 81.
32. Northrop Frye, *T. S. Eliot* (London & Edinburgh: Oliver and Boyd, 1963).
33. David E. Jones, *The Plays of T. S. Eliot* (London: Routlege & Kegan Paul, 1960), p. 59.
34. Ibid., p. 62
35. Ibid., pp. 62 and 67.
36. Ibid., p. 87.

Bibliography

The most useful and extensive bibliography of typology was compiled by Sacvan Bercovitch : 'Annotated Bibliography', in Sacvan Bercovitch (ed.), *Typology and Early American Literature* (Amherst: University of Massachusetts Press, 1972), pp. 245–337. I have learned from Professor Bercovitch that unfortunately his invaluable compilation has never been updated. Bibliographies in recent anthologies on typology and literature are informative – in English: Earl Miner (ed.), *Literary Uses of Typology from the Late Middle Ages to the Present* (Princeton: Princeton University Press, 1977); in German: Volker Bohn (ed.), *Typologie Internationale Beitrage zur Poetik* (Frankfurt am Main: Suhrkamp, 1988); in Hungarian: Tibor Fabiny (ed.), *A tipologiai szimbolizmus* (Szeged: Attila Jozsef University, 1988). Further bibliographies: Hugh T. Keenan's 'A Check List on Typology and English Medieval Literature through 1972', in *Studies in the Literary Imagination*, 8 (1975): 159–66, is selected and limited. The bibliographies attached to the books of D. L. Baker (1976) and R. M. Davidson (1981) are helpful. P. J. Korschin's 'Typology : A Bibliographical Essay' as the last chapter of his book (1982) offers also a useful guide. My list below is also selective. I have organized my material under four headings: 1. Typology in the Bible; 2. Typology in the History of Hermeneutics; 3. Typology in Art; 4. Typology in Literature.

1 TYPOLOGY IN THE BIBLE

Anderson, B. W., 'Exodus Typology in Second Isaiah' in *Israel's Prophetic Heritage. Essays in Honor of James Muilenberg*, ed. B. W. Anderson and W. Harrelson (New York: Harper and Bros, 1962), pp. 177–95.

Baker, D. L., *Two Testaments One Bible: A Study of Some Modern Solutions to the Theological Problem of the Relationship Between the Old and the New Testaments* (Leicester: Inter-Varsity Press, 1976).

—— 'Typology and the Christian Use of the Old Testament', in *Scottish Journal of Theology* 29 (1976): 137–57.

Barr, James, *Old and New in Interpretation: A Study of Two Testaments* (London: SCM Press, 1966).

Brown, R. E., *The Sensus Plenior of Sacred Scripture* (Baltimore: St. Mary's University, 1955).

—— 'Sensus Plenior in the Last Ten Years', *Catholic Biblical Quarterly*, 25 (1963): 262–85.

—— and Sandra M. Schneiders, 'Hermeneutics', in *The New Jerome Biblical Commentary*, ed. R. E. Brown, Joseph A. Fitzmeyer, Roland E. Murphy (New Jersey: Prentice Hall, 1990) 1146–65.

Bultmann, R., 'Ursprung und Sinn der Typologie als hermeneutischer Methode.' *Theologische Literaturzeitung* 75 (1975): 205–12.

Cahill, P. Joseph, 'The Unity of the Bible', in *Biblica*, 65, (1984): 404–11.

—— 'Hermeneutical Implications of Typology', in *Catholic Biblical Commentary*, 44 (1982): 266–81.

Charity, A. C. *Events and Their Afterlife: The Dialectics of Christian Typology in the Bible and Dante* (Cambridge: Cambridge University Press, 1966).

Childs, 'Prophecy and Fulfillment: A Study of Contemporary Hermeneutics', in *Interpretation* 12 (1958): 260–71.

Cope, Gilbert, *Symbolism in the Bible and the Church* (New York: Philosophical Library, 1959).

Danielou, Jean, *The Bible and Liturgy* (Notre Dame: Notre Dame of University Press, 1956).

Davidson, Richard M., *Typology in Scripture: A Study of Hermeneutical Typos Structure* (Michigan: Berrien Spring, 1981).

Dentan, Robert C., 'Typology – Its Use and Abuse', in *Anglican Theological Review*, 34 (1952): 211–17.

Edwards, Jonathan, *Images or Shadows of Divine Things*, ed. Perry Miller (New Haven: Yale University Press, 1948)

Ellis, Earle E., *Paul's Use of the Old Testament* (Grand Rapids: Eerdmans, 1957).

—— 'How the New Testament Uses the Old', in *New Testament Interpretations: Essays on Principles and Methods*, ed. I. Howard Marshall (Exeter: Paternoster Press, 1977).

Fairbairn, P., *The Typology of Scripture*, 2 vols, 6th edn (New York: Funk and Wagnalls, 1876).

Farrer, Austin, *A Study of St. Mark* (New York: Oxford University Press, 1952).

—— 'Typology' in *Expository Times* 67 (1956): 228–31.

Goppelt, Leonard, *Typos: Die typologische Deutung des Alten Testaments im Neuen* (Guterslo:, Gerd Mohn, 1939), reprint, enlarged edition, (Darmstadt: Wissenschaftliche Buchgesellschaft, 1966) In English: *Typos: The Typological Interpretation of the Old Testament in the New*, trans. Donald H. Madvig (Grand Rapids: Eerdmans, 1982).

Goulder, Michael D., *Type and History in Acts* (London: SPCK, 1964).

Grelot, Pierre, 'Les figures bibliques', in *Nouvelle revue théologique* 84 (1962): 561–78, 673–98. English abridgement in *Theology Digest*, 14 (1966): 8–13.

Guild, William, *Moses Unveiled: or Those Figures which Served unto the Pattern and Shadow of Heavenly Things* (London: 1620).

Hays, Richard B., *Echoes of Scripture in the Letter of Paul* (New Haven, London: Yale University Press, 1989).
Hebert, Arthur G., *The Throne of David: A Study of the Fulfilment of The Old Testament in Jesus Christ and His Church* (London: Faber and Faber, 1941).
Hummel, H. D., 'The Old Testament Basis of Typological Interpretation', in *Biblical Research*, 9 (1964): 38–56.
Keach, Benjamin, *Tropologia: A Key to Open Scripture Metaphors Together with the Types of the Old Testament* (London: 1681), reprinted as *Preaching from the Types and Metaphors of the Bible* (Grand Rapids: Kregel Publ., 1972).
Lampe, G. W. H. and Woollcombe, K. J., *Essays on Typology* (London: SCM Press, 1957).
—— 'Hermeneutics and Typology', *London Quarterly and Holborn Review* 190 (1965): 17–25.
LaSor, William S., 'Prophecy, Inspiration and *Sensus Plenior*', in *Tyndale Bulletin* 29 (1978): 49–60.
—— 'The *Sensus Plenior* and Biblical Interpretation', in *Scripture Tradition and Interpretation*, ed. W. Ward Gasque and William S. LaSor (Grand Rapids: Eerdmans, 1978) pp. 260–77.
Lubac, Henri de, '"Typologie" et "allegorisme"', in *Recherches de science religieuse*, 34 (1947): 180–226.
Marks, Herbert, 'Pauline Typology and Revisionary Criticism', in *Journal of the American Academy of Religion*, LII (1984): 71–92.
Mather, Samuel, *The Figures and Types of the Old Testament* (Dublin: 1681) Reprinted and edited by M. I. Lowance (New York and London: Johnson reprint Corporation, 1969)
Moo, Douglas J., 'The Problem of the *Sensus Plenior*', in *Hermeneutics Authority and Canon*, ed. D. A. Carson, John D. Woodbridge (Grand Rapids: Zondervan, 1986).
Markus, R. D., 'Presuppositions of the Typological Approach to Scripture', in *Church Quarterly Review*, 1858 (1957): 442–51.
Oss, Douglas A., 'Canon as Context : The Function of the *Sensus Plenior* in Evangelical Hermeneutics', in *Grace Theological Journal*, 9 (1988): 105–27.
Rad, Gerhard von, 'Typologische Auslegung des Alten Testaments', *Evangelische Theologie* 12 (1952–53): 17–33. English translation by John Bright in *Interpretation*, 15 (1961): 174–92; repr. in *Essays in Old Testament Hermeneutics*, ed. Claus Westermann (Richmond VA: John Knox Press, 1963) pp. 174–92.
—— *Theologie des alten Testaments* Vol. II. (Munchen: Kaiser, 1960), pp. 17–39. In English, *Old Testament Theology II: The Theology of Israel's Prophetic Traditions* (Edinburgh: Oliver & Boyd, 1965).
Robinson, J. M., 'Scripture and Theological Method: A Protestant Study in *Sensus Plenior*' in *Catholic Biblical Quarterly*, 27 (1965): 6–27.

Smart, James p. 'Typology, Allegory and Analogy', in *The Interpretation of Scripture* (London: SCM, 1961).
Stek, John H. 'Biblical Typology Yesterday and Today', in *Calvin Theological Journal*, 5 (1970): 133-62.
Taylor, Thomas, *Christ Revealed Or the Old Testament Explained* (London: 1635) A Facsimile Reproduction with an Inroduction by Raymond A. Anselment, Scholars Facsimile Reprints (New York: Delmar, 1979).

2 TYPOLOGY IN THE HISTORY OF HERMENEUTICS

Avis P. (ed.), *The Study and Use of The Bible The History of Christian Theology*, Vol. 2 (Grand Rapids: Eerdmans, 1988).
Caplan, Harry, 'The Four Senses of Scriptural Interpretation and the Medieval Theory of Preaching', in *Speculum*, 4 (1929): 282-90.
Danielou, Jean, *From Shadow to Reality: Studies in the Biblical Typology of the Fathers* (London: Westminster, Newman, 1960) [French: *Sacramentum Futuri*, 1950].
—— *Origen* (New York: Sheed and Ward, 1955).
Ellis, Earle E., *Prophecy and Hermeneutics in the Early Church* (Tubingen: J. B. Mohr, Paul Sibeck, 1978).
Fishbane, Michael, *Biblical Interpretation in Ancient Israel* (Oxford: Clarendon Press, 1985), pp. 350-79.
Froehlich, Karlfried, *Biblical Interpretation in the Early Church* (Philadelphia: Fortress Press, 1984).
Grant, Robert M., *A Short History of the Interpretation of the Bible* (New York: Macmillan, 1963).
Henschel, Martin 'Figuraldeutung und Geschichtlichkeit', in *Kerygma und Dogma*, 5 (1959): 306-17.
Longenecker, Richard N., *Biblical Exegesis on the Apostolic Period* (Grand Rapids: Eerdmans, 1975)
Lubac, Henri de, *Exegese médievale: les quatre sens de l'Ecriture*, 2 vols (Paris: Aubier, 1959-1964)
Matthei, Angelika, *Typologisches in Luthers deutschen Schriften*, Unpublished Thesis (Munster, 1983).
Müller, Hans Martin 'Die Figuraldeutung und die Anfange der Geschichtstheologie Luthers', in *Kerygma und Dogma*, 7 (1961): 221-36.
Preus, James Samuel, *From Shadow to Promise: Old Testament Interpretation from Augustine to the Young Luther* (Cambridge, Mass: The Belknap Press of Harvard University Press, 1969)
Schmidt, Margot (ed.), together with C. F. Geyer, *Typus Symbol Allegorie bei den osltlischen Vatern und ihren Parralelen im Mittelalter*, Eichstatter Betitrage, Band 4 (Regensburg: Pustet, 1982)
Smalley, Beryl, *The Study of The Bible in the Middle Ages* (Oxford: Oxford University Press, 1941).

Woollcombe, K. J., 'The Biblical Origins and Patristic Development of Typology', in G. W. H. Lampe and K. J. Woollcombe (eds), *Essays in Typology* (London: SCM Press, 1957).

3 TYPOLOGY IN ART

Bloch, Peter, 'Typologie' in Engelbert Kirschbaum, *et al.*, *Lexicon der christlichen Ikonographie* Vol IV (Rome: Herder, 1968–74), pp. 395–403.

—— Peter, 'Typologische Kunst', in *Lex et Sacramentum im Mittelalter* Miscellenea Medievalia 6, ed. P. Wilpert (Berlin: Walter de Gruyter, 1969) pp. 127–42.

Buschhausen, Helmut, 'The Klosterneuburg Altar of Nicholas of Verdun: Art, Theology and Politics', *Journal of the Warburg and Courtauld Institutes*, 37 (1974): 1–32.

Cavinnes, Madeline, *The Early Stained Glass of Canterbury Cathedral circa 1175–1220* (Princeton: Princeton University Press, 1977).

Henry, Avril (ed.), *The Mirour of Mans Saluatione a Middle English Translation of Speculum Humanae Salvationis* (London: Scolar Press, 1986).

—— (ed.) *Biblia Pauperum. A Facsimile and Edition* (London: Scolar Press, 1987).

Hollander, Hans, '"inwendig voller Figur" Figurale und typologische Denkformen in der Malerei', in Bohn, Volker (eds), *Typologie Internationale Betrage zur Poetik* (Frankfurt am Main: 1988), pp. 166–205.

James, M. R., 'Pictor in Carmine', in *Archaeologia Society of Antiquarians of London*, 94 (1951): 141–166.

Künstle, Karl, *Ikonographie der christlichen Kunst*, 2 vols (Freiburg: Herder, 1926, 1928)

Landow, George P., *William Holmann Hunt and Typological Symbolism* (New Haven and London: Yale University Press, 1979)

Mâle, Emile, *Religious Art in France in the Late Middle Ages: A Study of Medieval Iconography and Its Sources* (Princeton: Princeton University Press, 1986) [First edn 1908]

—— *Religious Art in France: The Thirteenth Century* (Princeton: Princeton University Press, 1986) [6th edn Paris, 1925]

Ohly, Friedrich, *Gesetz und Evangelium: zur Typologie bei Luther und Lucas Cranach. Zum Blutstrahl der Gnade in der Kunst* (Munster: Aschendorf, 1985).

Panofsky, Erwin (ed. and trans.), *Abbot Suger on the Abbey Church of St.-Denis and Its Art Treasures* (Princeton: Princeton University Press, 1946).

Reau, Louis, *Iconographie de l'art chrétien*, 6 vols (Paris: Presses Universitaires de France, 1955–59).

Röhrig, Floridus, *Der Verduner Altar* (Vienna: Herold, 1955).

—— 'Rota in Medio Rotae. Ein Typologischer Zyklus aus Osterreich', *Jahrbuch des Stiftes Klosterneuburg* NF 5 (Klosterneuburg: Klosterneuburger Buch-und Kunstverlag, 1965).

Schiller, Gertrud, *Ikonographie der christlichen Kunst*, Vols. I and II (London: Lund Humphries, 1971).

Soltész, Erzsébet, *Biblia Pauperum: facsimile Edition of the Forty-Leaf Blockbook in the Library of the Esztergom Cathedral*, trans. Lily Halapy (Budapest: Corvina, 1967).

Watson Arthur, *The Early Iconography of the Tree of Jesse* (London: Oxford University Press, 1934)

Wayment, Hilary, *The Windows of King's College Chapel Cambridge*, Corpus Vitrearum Medii Aevi, Great Britain, Suppl. No.1 (London: Oxford University Press for the British Academy, 1972).

Wilson, Adrian and Joyce Lancester Wilson, *A Medieval Mirror Speculum Humanae Salvationis 1324–1500* (Berkeley: California University Press, 1985).

4 TYPOLOGY IN LITERATURE

Auerbach, Erich, 'Figurative Texts Illustrating Certain Passages of Dante's *Commedia*', in *Speculum*, 21 (1946): 474–89.

—— *Typologische Motive in der mittelalterlichen Literatur. Schriften und Vortrage des Petrarca-Instituts Köln* (2. Krefeld, Scherpe, 1953).

—— 'Figura', trans. Ralph Manheim, in *Scenes from Drama of European Literature* (New York: Merridian, 1959). First published in German in *Archivum Romanicum*, 1938.

—— 'Typological Symbolism in Medieval Literature', in *Yale French Studies*, 9 (1965): 3–10.

—— *Mimesis: The Representation of Reality in Western Literature*, trans. Williard Trask (Princeton: Princeton University Press, 1953)

Bercovitch, Sacvan, 'Typology in Puritan New England; The Williams-Cotton Controversy Reassessed', in *American Quarterly* 19 (1967): 165–91.

—— (ed.) *Typology and Early American Literature* (Amherst: University of Massachusetts Press, 1972).

—— *The Puritan Origins of the American Self* (New Haven: Yale University Press, 1975).

—— *The American Jeremiad* (Madison: University of Wisconsin Press, 1978);

—— 'The Typology of America's Mission', in *American Quarterly*, 30 (1978): 135–55.

Berkeley, David S., *Inwrought With Figures Dim: A Reading of Milton's 'Lycidas'* (The Hague, Paris: Mouton, 1974)

—— 'Some Misapprehensions of Christian Typology in Recent Literary Scholarship', in *Studies in English Literature*, 18 (1978): 3–12.

Bohn, Volker (ed.), *Typologie. Internationale Beitrage zur Poetik* (Frankfurt am Main: Suhrkamp Verlag, 1988).

Brumm, Ursula, *American Thought and Religious Typology* (New Brunswick, New Jersey: Rutgers University Press, 1970).

Clark, Ira, *Christ Revealed: The History of Neotypological Lyric in the English Renaissance* (Gainesville: University of Florida Press, 1981)

Collins, J. Patrick, 'Typology, Criticism and Medieval Drama: Some Observations on the Method', *Comparative Drama* 10 (1976): 298–313.

Curtius, Ernst R. *European Literature and the Latin Middle Ages*, trans. Williard Trask (London: Routlege and Kegan Paul, 1953).

Frye, Northrop, 'The Typology of Paradise Regained', *Modern Philology*, 53 (1956): 227–38.

—— *Anatomy of Criticism: Four Essays* (New Jersey: Princeton University Press, 1957).

—— *The Great Code: The Bible and Literature* (London: Routlege & Kegan Paul, 1982).

—— *The Bible and Literature. A Personal View from Northrop Frye*, Thirty video programs with manuals. Exec. prod. Bob Rogers (Toronto: Media Center, 1982–83)

Galdon, J. *Typology in 17th Century Literature* (Hague, Paris: Mouton, 1975).

Genette, Gerard, *Figures of Literary Discourse*, trans. Alan Sheridan, Introd. Marie-Rose Logan (New York: Columbia Press, 1982).

Hoefer, Hartmut, *Typologie im Mittelalter. Zur Übertragbarkeit typologischer Interpretation auf weltliche Dichtung* (Goppingen: Kummerle, 1971).

Hurrel, John Dennis, 'The Figural Approach to Medieval Drama', *College English*, 26 (1965): 598–604.

Keenan, Hugh T. 'A Check-List on Typology and English Medieval Literature through 1972', in *Studies in Literary Imagination*, 8 (1975): 159–66.

Kolve, V. A., *The Play Called Corpus Christi* (Stanford: Stanford University Press, 1965).

Korschin Paul J. *Typologies in England 1650–1820* (Princeton: Princeton University Press 1982).

Krouse, F. M., *Milton's Samson and the Christian Tradition* (Princeton: Princeton University Press, 1949).

Landow, George P., *Victorian Types Victorian Shadows: Biblical Typology in Victorian Literature Art and Thought* (London: Routledge & Kegan Paul, 1980).

Leiter, Louis H., 'Typology, Paradigm and Image in the York Creation of Adam and Eve', *Drama Survey* 7 (1968–69): 113–33.

Lewalski, Barbara K, *Milton's Brief Epic* (Providence R.I., London: Brown University Press, 1966)

—— 'Typological Symbolism and the 'Progress of the Soul' in Seventeenth Century Literature', in *Literary Uses of Typology from the*

Late Middle Ages to the Present, ed. Earl Miner (Princeton: Princeton University Press, 1977), pp. 79–114.
—— *Protestant Poetics and Seventeenth Century Religious Lyric* (Princeton: Princeton University Press, 1979).
Lowance, Mason I. Jr, 'Typology and the New England Way: Cotton Mather's Exegesis', *Early American Literature*, 4 (1969): 15–37.
—— *The Language of Canaan. Metaphor and Symbol in New England from the Puritans to the Transcendentalist* (Cambridge, Mass., London: Harvard University Press, 1980).
MacCallum, H. R., 'Milton and the Figurative Interpretation of the Bible', *University of Toronto Quarterly*, 31 (1962): 397–415.
Mabee, Charles, 'The Violence of American Typological Revisionism', in *Forum*, Vol. 5 (1989): 3–19.
Madsen, William G., 'Earth the Shadow of Heaven. Typological Symbolism in *Paradise Lost*', in *PMLA*, 75 (1960): 519–26.
—— *From Shadowy Types to Truth: Studies in Milton's Symbolism* (New Haven: Yale University Press, 1968)
Meyers, W. E., *A Figure Given: Typology in the Wakefield Plays* (Pittsburgh: Duquesne University Press, 1970).
Miner, Earl (ed.), *Literary Uses of Typology from the Late Middle Ages to the Present* (Princeton: Princeton University Press, 1977).
Müller, Marcel, 'Prafiguration und Romanstruktur in *A la recherche du temps perdu*', in Bohn, Volker (eds), *Typologie, op. cit., pp. 401–62*.
Ohly, Friedrich, 'Vom Geistigen Sinn des Wortes in Mittelalter', in *Schriften zur Mittelalterlichen Bedeutungsforschung* (Darmstadt: Wissenschaftliche Buchgesellschaft, 1977) pp. 1–31. First published in *Zeitschrift fur deutsches Altertum und deutsche Literatur*, 89 (1958–59): 1–23.
—— 'Synagoge und Ecclesia. Typologisches im mittelalterlicher Dichtung', in *Schriften*, pp. 312–37.
—— 'Halbbiblische und ausserbiblische Typologie' in *Schriften*, pp. 361–99.
—— 'Skizzen zur Typologie im spateren Mittelalter, in *Medium Aevum deutsch. Beitrage zur detschen Literatur des hohen und spaten Mittelalters. Festschrift Kurt Ruh zum 65. Geburtstag (Tubingen: 1979), pp. 251–310*.
—— 'Typologie als Denkform der Geschichtsbetrachtung', in Bohn, Volker (eds), *Typologie op. cit. 22–63*.
—— 'Typologische Figuren aus Natur und Mythus', in Haug, Walter (ed.), *Formen und Funktionen der Allegorie* (Stuttgart: J. B. Metzlersche Verlagsbuchhandlung, 1979), pp. 126–66.
Owst, Gerald R., *Literature and Pulpit in Medieval England: A Neglected Chapter in the History of English Letters and of the English People* (Oxford: Blackwell, 1961; 2nd edn).
Pickering, Frederick P. *Literature and Art of the Middle Ages* (London: Macmillan, 1970).

Robertson, D. W., Jr. 'The Question of Typology and the Wakefield *Mactatio Abel*', in *American Benedictine Review*, 25 (1974): 157–73.

Salter, Elisabeth, 'Medieval Poetry and the Figural View of Reality', in *Proceedings of the British Academy*, 54 (1968): 73–92.

Schröder, Werner, 'Zum Typologie-Begriff und Typologie-Verstandnis in der mediavistischen Literaturwissenschaft', in Scholler, Harald (eds), *The Epic in Medieval Society Aesthetic and Moral Values* (Tübingen: 1957).

Tuve, Rosemond, *A Reading of George Herbert* (Chicago: University of Chicago Press, 1953)

Woolf, Rosemary, 'The Effect of Typology on the English medieval Plays of Abraham and Isaac', in *Speculum*, 32, (1957): 805–25.

—— *The English Mystery Plays* (Berkely and Los Angeles: University of California Press, 1972).

Williams, Arnold, 'Typology and the Cycle Plays, Some Criteria', in *Speculum* 43 (1968): 677–84.

Ziolkowski, Theodore, *Fictional Transfigurations of Jesus* (Princeton: Princeton University Press, 1972).

—— 'Some Features of Religious Figuralism in Twentieth-Century Literature', in Miner (ed.), *Literary Uses of Typology*, pp. 345–369.

Index

Abraham-typology 68–9
Adamic-typology 67–8
Alan of Lille 111
Allegory 18, 28–8, 33–4, 112, 115
  vs. typology 85
Allegorical interpretation
  See, Interpretation
Alter, Robert 50
St Ambrose 117
analogia entis 113
analogia fidei 113
antitypos 17
Anti-visual prejudice 79, 82, 111
St Anselm of Canterbury 126
Apocalypse 43, 76
Appropriation 11, 42–4, 77, 113
  swallowing the book 76–7, 113, 136
Aquinas, Thomas 27, 104
Architext
  See, Text, theories of
Art of God
  See, Typology
Atonement 126–8
  deception of Satan 127
Atoning sacrifice 71
St Augustine 117
Auerbach, Erich 3, 4, 15–16, 25–6, 43–4, 114–15
  Mimesis 15
  'Figura', 4, 16
  on figural interpretation 25, 114

Bach, Johann Sebastian 83
Baptism 68
Battenhouse, Roy W. 126
Bercovitch, Sacvan 3
Bevington, David 119
Biblia Pauperum 3, 93–103, 107–10, 116–18, 122
  aim and structure of 94–100
  use of typology in 96–100
  reading of pictures in 100–3

  source of sermons 100–3
  rewriting of 109–10
Biblical language 13–26, 39, 74
Blake, William 10
Bloom, Harold 11, 43
Book, symbol of 74–7, 113
Bouts, Dirck 105, 109
Brome-plays
  See, Non-cycle-plays
Brown, Raymond E. 36–7
Brumm, Ursula 3
Bultmann, Rudolf 12, 14, 25, 47
Buschhausen, Helmut 92–3

Cahill, Joseph P. 9
Canonical criticism 39
Cassian, John 28
Causality 7
Charity, A. C. 3, 55, 58, 66, 112
Chaucer, Geoffrey 129
  The Clerk's Tale 129
Chester-cycle
  See, Cycle-plays
Childs, Brevard S. 9, 22, 29–30
Chrysostom, John 33, 116
St Clement 18, 28, 32
Christianity
  attitude to images 79–80
Circumcision 67
Coghill, Nevill 128–9
Comic form 12–31
  fulfilment in 131
Coppens, Joseph 37
Corpus Christi cycle 116–17
Corpus Christi day, 116
Covenant-typology 67–9
Cranach, Lucas, 83
Creation-typology 64–5, 67–8
Cullmann, Oscar 47–7
Cult 58
Cycle-plays 116–22
  Chester 118–22
  York 118

159

Townely 118
Ludus Coventriae, 118

Dante 31, 129
Divine Comedy 129
Davidson, Clifford 79
Day of Atonement 71
Deception of Satan
 See, Atonement
deigma 18, 73
De Voraigne, Jacobus 104
deus absconditus 123
Diodore of Tarsus 33
Donne, John 82
Dublin-play
 See, Non-cycle-plays
Dürer, Albrecht 83

Ebed-Jahve songs 61–3
Ebeling, Gerhard, 37
Ellis, Earl E. 67
ego
 dissapearance of 42–4, 77
Eliot, T. S. 10
 Murder in the Cathedral
  113–14, 131–6
 'Poetry and Drama' 132
Emblematic stage 122
Enlightenment 10
Esmeijer, Anna, C. 84
Eusebius 80–1
Exemplification
 See Parable
Eye vs. Ear 79–80
Everyman 132

Fairbairn, Parick 48
figura 1, 4, 16–20, 115
Figural interpretation 25, 14, 123
 vs. allegorical interpretation
  114
 reality principle in 115
Figuralism
 See, typology
Figurative reading 113, 129
Figures Fulfilled in the New Testament
 Abraham 68–9
 Adam 67

Balaam 73
Cain 73
Core, 73
Flood, 73
High-Priest 70–2
Israel 69–70
King 60–1
Lamb 64–6, 73–7
Lion 73–77, 92
Passover 64–6
Prophet 59–60
Sodom and Gomorrha 73
Son of Man 61
Stone 72
Suffering Servant 61–2
Twelve tribes 63
Fishbane, Michael 48, 53, 56
Flavius, Josephus 61
forma perfectior 24
Frye, Northrop 1, 3–9, 14–15,
 30–1, 43–4, 46, 51–2, 58, 76–7,
 112, 122, 128, 135
 Anatomy of Criticism, 5
 Fearful Symmetry 5
 Great Code, The 1, 4, 5–7
 Return of Eden, The 5
Fulfil 20–3
Fulfilment 2, 22–3, 58–77, 111,
 113–14
 comedy, in 131
 recreation 114
 reading 136
Fulfilment-language 16, 26, 29, 57
Fullness of language 16
Fundamentalism 26

Gadamer, Hans Georg 10, 37
Genette, Gerard 114
Gombrich, Ernst 79
Goppelt, Leonard 12, 25–6, 46–7,
 60–2, 64–5, 68
Goulder, M. D. 67
Groseclose, Sidney 91
Grünewald 83

Heilsgeschichte
 See, Salvation history
Henry, Avril 94–5, 99, 104–5, 108
Hermeneutics

Index

Biblical 26–39
Visual 83–5
Dramatic 115–22, 137
Historia Scolastica 101, 104
hypotyposis 18
hypodeigma 18, 73

Icon 78
Iconoclasm 79, 80, 82–3
  Byzantine Christianity 80
  Middle Ages 80
  Reformation 81–3
Iconography 79
Idolatry 79–80, 101
Images 82–3
  debates about 80
  idolatrous 84
  function of 84
  therapeutic 84
  veneration of 80, 83
Imitation
  See, Typology
imitatio Christi 137
Inspiration 39–42
  postcritical theory of 40–42
Intention
  authorial vs. textual 43
Interpretation 23, 40, 42–3, 123, 137
  deciphering symbols 114
  allegorical vs. figurative 114
  visual images 84
Interpenetration 44, 75, 85
Intertextuality 2, 76, 107, 114, 136
Irenaeus 56
Isidore of Seville 85
Israel-typology 69–70
James, M. R. 86
Jones, David E. 134–5
Jonson, Ben 129
Josipovici, Gabriel 111

Karlstadt, Andreas Bodenstein 82–3
Kermode, Frank 3
kerygma 7, 14, 48, 78
Kierkegaard, Søren 7, 10, 134
Klosterneuburg Altar 87–93, 99, 107–10, 117–18
  structure of 88–92
  sources of 92–3
  designer of 93
Knight, G. Wilson 124–5, 129
Kolve, V. A. 116
Korshin, P. J. 3
Kristeva, Julia 114

Language 13–26
  phases of 7
Landow, George 3
LaSor, William Sanford 37–9
Legenda Aurea 104
Lewalski, Barbara Kiefer 3
Lion and Lamb 35, 44, 73–7
Literal sense
  See, Senses of Scripture
Literal truth 15
Ludus Coventriae
  See, Cycle plays
Luther, Martin 81–3, 86
  views on language of 82–3

Mâle, Emile 4, 103, 105, 109
Meaning 26, 40
  polysemous 30–2
  sententia 34–5
  sensus plenior 35–9
  surplus of 23–4, 114–15, 123, 130, 137
  theoria 19, 32–4
Marcion 11–12, 32
Marx, Karl 8
Melito of Sardis
  On Pascha 116
Meta-comedy 130, 132–7
Metaphor 24
Metaphorical language 74
Miles, Margaret 81–4
Miller, Perry 3
Milton, John 3, 5, 19, 44, 77, 82, 112–13, 122
  Paradise Lost 19
Miner, Earl 112
Mirour of Mans Saluacione
  See, *Speculum Humanae Salvationis, Middle English translation of*,
Myth 6, 17,

Nazi-Bible 12
Neoplatonism 115
New Hermeneutics 37
Nicholas of Verdun 88, 93
Nietzsche, Friedrich 10
Non-cycle plays
  Brome 118–19
  Dublin (Northampton) 118

Ohly, Friedrich 3
On Pascha
  See, Melito of Sardis
Ong, Walter 78
Origen 18, 28, 32–3, 117

Panofsky, Erwin 79
Parable 18, 33, 115–16
  atonement of 126
  drama as 124
  exemplification 115
  Ricoeur's idea of 125
  Two Debtors 125
  Unmerciful Servant 125
Peter Comestor 101, 104–5
Phases of Language
  See, Language
Phases of Revelation
  See, Revelation
Philo 32
Pictor in Carmine 86–7, 92
pictura
  antitype as 84
  text as 85
pictura quasi scriptura 84
Pilgrim Fathers 3
Plato 9
Polysemous meaning,
  See, Meaning
Populist literalism 30
Postcritical theory of inspiration
  See, Inspiration
Postfiguration 112–45
Prefiguration 116
  fulfilment of 136
Pre-Raphaelites 3
Primogeniture 50–2
Promos and Cassandra
  See, Whetstone
Prophecy 92, 37

Puritans 80

Quadriga
  See, Senses of Scripture

Rashi 34
Reader 76–7
Reading 39–44
  appropriation, as 11, 42–4
  images 85
  inspiration, as 40–2
  recreation, as 41, 77–8
  re-enactment, as 113
  rewriting, as 41
  usurpation, in 11, 43
Reality-principle
  See, Figural interpretation
Recreation 15, 26, 41, 77–8, 114
  fulfilment, in 114
Re-enactment
  See, reading, typology
Reformation
  views of images, of 81–3
Remnant 56
Revelation,
  book of 73–7
  phases, of 7
Ricoeur, Paul 8, 10, 14–16, 23,
  42–4, 63, 77, 79, 123, 125
Ripa, Cesare 79
Robinson, J. M. 37
Roston, Murray 112–13
Rota in medio rotae 87, 92
Röhrig, Floridus 87

Salvation history 27, 46–7
School of Alexandria 18, 28, 32–3
School of Antioch 18, 32–4
Scriptura
  type, as 84
Senses of Scripture 27–30, 34–5
  sensus litteralis 29
  sensus originalis 29
  sensus plenior
  See, meaning
  sententia
  See, meaning
Shakespeare, William 7

Measure for Measure 113, 122–31
 comedy, as 129
 parable, as 125–36
 reality-fallacy, in 130
 The Merchant of Venice 124
Sheppard, Gerald T. 9
Sidney, Philip Sir 129
skia 20
Sign 60, 111
Smalley, Beryl 34
Speculum Humanae Salvationis 96, 103–9, 116
 author, of 103–4
 intertext, in 107
 purpose, of 104
 structure, of 104–5
 Middle English Translation, of 104
 reading of a chapter, in 105–7
 sermons, used as 105–7
Spiritual sense,
 See, senses of Scripture
Steigerung 27, 47, 59, 64, 73–4, 137
Stone-typology 72
 cornerstone 72
 foundation stones 63, 72
 living stone 72
 rejected stone 72
 rock 70, 72,
 stone cut out without hands 72
 stumbling stone 72
Subfulfilment 66, 112
Supertext
 See, text, theories, of
Surplus of meaning
 See, meaning
Swallowing the book
 See, appropriation
Symbol 11, 123

tableau vivant 122
Tertullian 23, 80, 117
Text, theories of 42–3, 78
 architext 114–15
 supertext 114–15
Temple 57
theoria
 See, meaning
Townely cycle,

 See, Cycle-plays
Transparency,
 definition, of 75
 life, of 44, 77
 opaque, vs. 44, 115
 texts 75
 world 75
Travis, Peter W. 122
Type-scenes 50–1
Typology
 art of God, as 116, 133
 construction of the Bible, as 46
 contemporarization, as 55
 cult, as 58
 fusion of events, as 54, 61, 63–4, 71–2, 74
 God's design, as 116
 Hebrew Bible, in 48–9
 hermeneutical method, as 70
 imitation, as 137
 New Testament, in 58–77
 new interpreted in terms of the old, as 49, 53, 55, 59, 76
 Old Testament, in 47–58
 reactualization of events, as 55
 recapitulation, as 56, 58, 69
 recurring patterns, as 49–53
 redivivus of earlier persons, as 59–60
 reenactment of a pattern, as 131
 reinterpretation, as 26
 reiteration, as 56
 renewal of covenant, as 50
 revisionary reading, as 26
 principle of unity, as 46–7
 prophecy, vs. 92
 salvation history, vs. 47,
 Stephen's narrative, in 66–7
 spiritual approach, as 70
 usurpation of Hebrew Bible, as 11, 43
Typological art 108–10
Typological dictionaries 85–6, 109
typos 1, 16–17, 23, 116
 See also, figura

umbra 20
Unity of the Bible 9, 45–7

Usurpation of Hebrew Bible
  See, typology
ut pictura poesis 79

Valerianus Maximus 108
Van der Weyden, Roger 105
Van Eyck, Jan 105
Verbality vs. visuality 78–85, 100
Vincent de Beauvais 128–9
Visual exegesis 83–5
Visuality vs. verbality
  See, Verbality vs. visuality
Vogels, Walter 40–2

Von Rad, Gerhard 3, 46–8

Whetstone, George
  Promos and Cassandra 124
Wilson, Adrian 103–4
Wilson, Joyce Lancester 103–4

York cycle
  See, Cycle-plays

Zwingli, Ulrich 82
Zwischengesänge 93